The Incompleteness Book II

Writing Back & Thinking Forward

Edited by
Julia Prendergast
Eileen Herbert-Goodall
Jen Webb

The Incompleteness Book II: Writing Back and Thinking Forward

Recent Work Press

Canberra, Australia

Copyright © the authors, 2021

ISBN: 978-0-6451808-4-8 (paperback)

All rights reserved. This book is copyright. Except for private study, research, criticism or reviews as permitted under the Copyright Act, no part of this book may be reproduced, stored in a retrieval system, or transmitted in any form by any means without prior permission. Enquiries should be addressed to the publisher.

Cover photograph, design and typesetting: Thomas Hamlyn-Harris

recentworkpress.com

RECENT
WORK
PRESS

Contents

Introduction, *Julia Prendergast*	1
The Op Shop Volunteer, *Alberta Natasia Adji*	5
A Year On, *Eugen Bacon*	7
Innovators, *Eugen Bacon*	8
Advice to Hansel and Gretel, *Roxanne 'Therese' Bodsworth*	9
The Summer of Water, *Donna Lee Brien*	10
Thrip like fingertips, *Didem Caia*	11
Employable Me, *Aidan Coleman*	12
The Affair, *Shady Cosgrove*	13
Immigrant Allegiance, *Shady Cosgrove*	14
Wellington peonies December 2020, *Lynn Davidson*	15
From Scotland to New Zealand, *Lynn Davidson*	16
a timid database, *Dave Drayton*	17
cold feet, *Dave Drayton*	18
Nightingale, *Katrina Finlayson*	20
Velkommen Hjem, *Katrina Finlayson*	22
Centre Aisle, *Laura Fulton*	23
beyond the dark line of trees, *Jane Frank*	24
Poem for the End of Time, *Stephanie Green*	26
Rust, *Stephanie Green*	27
Refuge, *Rebecca Hamilton*	28
Rain, *Thomas Hamlyn-Harris*	29
Π, *Dominique Hecq*	30
Vigil, *Dominique Hecq*	32
City, *Paul Hetherington*	33
Tunnel, *Paul Hetherington*	33
A chart of the incompleteness of human experience, one year on, *Christine Howe*	34
The Last Time We Saw Each Other, *Anita Jawary*	35
Toxic Towers, *Sue Joseph and Anon*	36
Spent Ink, *Daniel Juckes*	37
Wings, *Helena Kadmos*	38
To Mauritius, *Dean Kerrison*	39
Childhood Dreaming, *Jeri Kroll*	40
Explorer on the Moon: 2021, *Joshua Lobb*	41
Year of Breath December 31, 2020, *Rose Lucas*	42
The Weather Up Here, *Mia Francesca Michelle McAuslan*	43

Rattus and Oxen, *Gay Lynch*	44
The Art of Letting Go, *Mario Daniel Martín*	46
Against Entropy, *Sam Meekings*	48
Murray's Covidictionary, *Peta Murray*	50
Two more weeks, *Lili Pâquet*	53
Pruning, *Mary Pomfret*	54
Inkling, *Mary Pomfret*	55
Firesky, *Julia Prendergast*	56
Self-flagellation and the Falls, *Peter Ramm*	58
Love is love in place, *Sandra Renew*	60
morning sickness, *Sarah Pearce*	62
Tethered, *Rachel Robertson*	63
Finding Home, *Deedle Rodriguez-Tomlinson*	64
Missing, *Hazel Smith*	66
Viral Year, *Hazel Smith*	67
My Untranquil Mouth, *Marion Pym Schaare*	68
Cut Flowers, *Shannon Sandford*	70
How We Live Now, *Dominic Symes*	71
The Gift after Czeslaw Milosz, *Dominic Symes*	72
The Story of the Watch, *Amelia Walker*	74
Prismatic: Fragments, Pieces, Splinters, *Annmaree Watharow with Ronnith Morris*	76
Another step in the cycle, *Jen Webb*	78
Back to where we started from, *Jen Webb*	78
The Tea-Room, First Day Back, *Rose Williamson*	79
(Un) Certainty, *Miriam Wei Wei Lo*	80
Leaving Lockdown: My Wish for You, *Kimberly K. Williams*	82
Ode: Facing the Light, *Dugald Williamson*	84
A Letter in Autumn, *Dugald Williamson*	85
The Seventh Day, *Christina Yin*	86
Bio notes	88

Introduction
Julia Prendergast

In April 2020, amidst the global pandemic of COVID-19, the Australasian Association of Writing Programs (AAWP), the peak academic body representing the discipline of Creative Writing in Australasia, sent out a call for contributions to a Special Issue of *TEXT—Journal of Writing and Writing Courses*. The theme of the Special Issue was *The in/completeness of human experience*. The collection was subsequently published as *The Incompleteness Book* (2020: Recent Work Press). Thanks to the generosity of Shane Strange, publisher at Recent Work Press, we have a follow-up collection. I begin in homage and gratitude to Shane, for providing us with the opportunity to come together as a community of practitioners.

Thank you to my fellow editors, Distinguished Professor Jen Webb and Dr Eileen Herbert-Goodall, for solidarity, for sharing the labour and the laughs, and co-revelling in the superb voices in this collection. We were deeply interested in capturing a composite picture of what people made of the prompt: the incompleteness of human experience, *one year on*. We asked contributors to write back and think forward, encouraging our fellow writers to consider what they had discarded; what they coveted more closely than ever; whether they had learned something, about themselves or more broadly. We were interested in a collective expression of: Where to, from here?

In the 2020 issue of *The Incompleteness Book* I flagged my obsession with the relationship between the haunting incompleteness of human experience and short form writing, as the lure for coming together as writers. I referred to Gordon Weaver who asks: 'in how small a space can [we] create the *felt presences* that animate successful stories [or poems]?' (1983: 228, emphasis added). I suggested that the world becomes groundless in the creative enactment of felt presences. The contributions to the second collection bolster my faith in this assumption. As was the case for the 2020 collection, the writing is somewhat obsessed with details and their place, in time. What strikes me in the submissions, this time, is the forever-tinged imagining of what had seemed 'sudden' (if not unprecedented or unexpected). We seem to be asking: *What does living with this for the foreseeable forever look like?*

My thinking is informed by 'Melbourne-time'. We have been in lockdown for more days than anywhere else in the world. I've been moved, throughout this period, by stories of caregiving in its various forms, so many people caught in a cycle of relentless care, behind-closed-doors, without assistance. I am acutely aware that I am extremely fortunate—this sickens me and makes me feel inordinately grateful. Overall, the past year has reminded me of when my children were little and I was, essentially, housebound. For many years I had a baby, as well as a number of young children. During those years I studied at night; during the day I would 'make things'. One of my daytime hobbies was to restore decrepit furniture. We live in an old house which, at that time, did not have bedroom robes. I would buy old furniture from the Salvos, sand the timber back to its raw state, and re-lacquer—the blissful rhythm of repetitive movement, the 'nothingness' activity that facilitates what Joanne Yoo describes as the 'unravel[ling] of flickers of truth and beauty that elude the rational mind' (Yoo 2021: 74). Furniture restoration was a task with a practical outcome, somewhere to house clothes and shoes, but it was something else, too—a way of marking days and weeks in acts of making, when time otherwise blended imperceptibly. In pandemia, I have been thinking and dreaming obsessively about those years of backyard furniture restoration, relentless caregiving—the loop of endless need and nowhere else to go, nowhere else to be. *Why?* The minutiae of our lives, now…

Across this timeless vortex I have filled my 'spare' time with projects like the incompleteness books—projects *like* furniture restoration—a privileged desperation to achieve practical outcomes that mark time meaningfully—a need to maintain connections to the storytellers and the poets. The incompleteness books feel like a quest for restoration: a communal 'sanding back' of our lived experience.

I woke last night, thinking: I must write this introduction. I scrawled a note to myself: glasspaper, flickers of truth and beauty. Glasspaper is the final stage of the sanding process in domestic furniture restoration. The paper is beautiful—like fine, gold-flecked sand. Sanding with glass paper between the coats of lacquer means that the furniture is smooth-shiny like glass, shiny enough to reflect the everyday, incompletely.

Across the submissions we see this: 'fleeting flickers of intuitive understanding [...] through a half light'—'bringing into *being* [...] *what is possible* and what has *yet to come*' (Yoo 2021: 74, 75, emphasis in original). Thank you, dear authors—for reminding us how, as the ground shifts at every turn, we might sustain ourselves, for capturing the flickering, halflit mystery of lived experience, in wild acts of making.

Julia Prendergast (on behalf of the editors of *The Incompleteness Book II*)

Works cited

Weaver G 1983 in R Shapard and J Thomas (eds), **Sudden Fiction. American Short-Short Stories**, Layton, Utah: Gibbs Smith, 223–24

Yoo J 2021 'Writing creatively to catch flickers of 'truth' and beauty', *New Writing* 18. 1: 74–83

The Op Shop Volunteer
Alberta Natasia Adji

It takes me ten minutes to find the entrance before I introduce myself to the cashier girl: Leslie. She calls Addie who appears from behind the staff room.

'Here's our new girl,' says Leslie.

'Hiya,' says Addie. 'Welcome,' she says, motioning for me to follow her.

We gather armfuls of clothes, pricing as we go: plain hangers for shirts and dresses, $25 and under, hangers with clips for pants, wooden hangers for top-end items.

Addie waves her hand over the shelves on my left. 'Here's where we keep our second-hand books, DVDs, cassette tapes and vinyl records—some are quite niche,' she says, pointing to *Gumnut Babies*.

She taps the glass case at the cashier counter. 'Here's our collection of curios—handbags, decorated tea sets, jewels.' She hands me two thin stainless steel keys. 'You will need these to open the cabinet.'

Later, as I attach a blue tag to a green mermaid dress, dazzling with sequins, Addie asks me where I am from.

'Indonesia,' I tell her. 'But not from Bali.'

'Oh, where then?'

'Surabaya, East Java,' I say. What about yourself? You a Perth local?'

'Nah,' she grins, 'Mount Gambier ... South Australia.'

'How long have you been here—in the op shop?'

'Three years ...'

I look up to find Addie is dressed in the hotdog costume. 'I'm on a roll!' She giggles and tap-dances around. I take her picture on my phone.

Leslie appears. Addie stops dancing and I put my phone back in my pocket.

'There's a new local case,' she says. 'Three-day lockdown as of midnight, tonight.'

We groan and get busy. Later, we realise somebody has nicked a couple of designer items—the frill sleeve long dress and cashmere jumper. I had my eye on the honey-coloured jumper to wear with my skinny jeans, but it was sixty dollars. I was waiting for payday.

'The thief is the woman with the purple hair,' says Leslie. 'Next time she comes in, I'm watching.'

'Do we call the cops?' I ask them.

Addie presses her lips. 'It's tricky.'

'It's not so tricky,' says Leslie. 'Only four items in the change room. And we check purple-hair on the way out.'

I reckon it's a moral dilemma since the whole thing's church charity. 'I reckon …' I say. But they're not listening. They're focused on the man at the door, his long hair pulled back in a bun, arms laden with donations.

A Year On
Eugen Bacon

He's the buck of a young team—200cm lanky. He's the long reach, front position. It's a good disposal, ball above ground. Centre clearance. He's outnumbered in a forward position that's hard to defend. Shoulder to shoulder, slam tackle. Carnage at ground level. Moments later, he anticipates on his toes. No one's looking. He's the rookie, only the recruit. Nice potential—not the star. He goes for the flyer, makes light the knock to the line. Again, the ball. A tough angle for a left-footer. A tweak of the ankle, the kick travels deep. It's a magnificent finish. Silence. Someone ruffles his hair. His mum who can't travel—he hopes she saw. A gold-eyed magpie in ebony and snow plumage lands on the ball, pecks at it.

    A year on it's about transition. Bounce. Bounce. A quick right.

    He twists in the air, glides in an arc despite the match up.

    'That's special!' whoops the commentator.

    The young buck lines the mark in a ripple of sound.

    It's all good—he welcomes the boos. The thunder of claps.

    Disdain in a stadium at half capacity is better than cardboard fans.

    His clumsy goal squeezes inside the posts.

Innovators
Eugen Bacon

We inherited dread and laboured to remember the independence of babes sat on
Naked grass, curious fingers touching rainbow leaf beetles that can never be pets.
We broke our daughters from strangers, dabbed at tiny palms with fluids that
Assured us with *Added Aloe Vera, 70% Alcohol, Kills 99.99% of Germs.*
Our new game, Rub-Your-Hands-Together, covered all surfaces
But it got into their eyes, their mouths, and they wailed.
We tutored them about masks and lockdowns,
Not bouncy winds and countryside photos.
We assembled words to tell about death
About death aboutdeathdeathdeath
What language speaks of life?

Advice to Hansel and Gretel
Roxanne 'Therese' Bodsworth

If you hear your father in discussion
with your stepmother about ditching
the two of you, so they have enough to eat,
ditch them first.

Don't worry
about filling your pockets
to leave a trail homewards,
not with pebbles or crumbs,
it's not a home you want to return to.

Get in first. You know
where the axe is kept
and have learned well how to wield it.
Get rid of them.
Hide their bodies in the outhouse.
Nobody will miss them
as nobody would have missed you
if you had been led
into the heart of the forest.

Run the farm yourself, you know how,
you've been doing all the chores
since you could walk.
And you won't need as much to stay fed
as those greedy sods with their pillow talk.
There are eggs, goat's milk, still a sack of spuds,
enough for two small children
and far better for you
than sweets and gingerbread.
Trust me on that one.

The Summer of Water
Donna Lee Brien

After two brutal summers of drought and bushfire, it has rained. And rained. And kept raining.

The ponds and dams are overflowing, with yabbies found astonishing distances from their homes. The creeks ran and reached the river, and it too flowed anew. Sometimes the creek is so high over the road, we have to make a one hundred-kilometre detour to get to town. Usually we stay home and drink tea on the front porch, listening to the river raging and watching our two hand-fed lambs, now fully-grown sheep, chase the dogs through the puddles in the driveway.

The paddocks which had dried to dirt first tinged green, and then erupted into fragile shoots which soon became lush growth. Now the horses are sleek and content, standing in pasture that reaches their full, rounded bellies. On sunny days, they take splashy baths in the dam, roll luxuriantly in the long grass and finally finish their toilette by thundering around the paddock, splattering each other with muddy clods.

Hundreds of thousands of litres of water are now safely stored in tanks around the house and woolshed, but drought habits are hard to shake. It has taken most of a year to not feel guilty when washing more than only the most necessary items or letting the dishwater run down the sink instead of saving it for the garden. We still can't let a tap run for any reason, ever.

It is easy to focus on the vivid greenery instead of the skeletal remains of the gums that succumbed to the dry, but they are legion, and many of the oldest and grandest perished. I also miss the rest of the sheep. We had to sell our small flock after the fire and, since the rain, very few young ewes have come onto the restocking market. With the endless water and piles of compost, our kitchen garden largely recovered, but a number of summer crops have not flourished. Many tomato and other flowers fell unpollinated, local beehives no doubt incinerated for hundreds of kilometres all around.

The most unwelcome visitors are the hordes of mice who all seem to want to live in the pantry. Field mice do, however, provide ready picnics for the kookaburras who, revelling in this season of water, hunt and gorge and then sing of their successes, their sunshiny laughter brightening the dampest day.

Thrip like fingertips
Didem Caia

Thrip like fingertips
Tap nervous on pages, spent and exhausted
Edges and moments of white page ready for
/flicks and /flurries.

Mind stops
What was I going for with this sentence?

Past tense,
Writing to pass the time
Thunder thrips of fingertips
Tap. Tap. Tap. Away.

Energy clots
How many words now?

Across the page a word here, a word there
Scurry, hurry, get it done
Like a torchlight over thrips
fingers flee. Like silent screams. In many directions.

Stomach knots (Knotted? No(t)ted? Note?)
Is there a right way anymore?

Employable Me
Aidan Coleman

The subject line 'Employable Me' keeps appearing in my inbox—and until it goes red or threatens to cut some family benefit, I'll continue to ignore it. It's one of a number of encouraging head-pats I've received since signing up to Job Seeker; that is, since I—like thousands of other casual academics—was cut adrift by COVID-induced austerity.

As a defence against shelf stacking (a job I excelled at pre-stroke) or working in childcare (the job alert they keep sending me because it sounds vaguely educational), I signed up with a disability employment provider, which for the purposes of anonymity I will refer to by the acronym DRAB.

Having a disability allows me to work for just 15 hours per week but it does not entitle me to search for fewer jobs. Each month—at DRAB's insistence—I bother ten unwitting employers, and because the jobs are improbable I don't try very hard: *I am a member of at least seven libraries and at some of them they know me well.*

I don't think DRAB has ever had a writer on its books, and I explain my vocation over the phone each Monday. When asked by my case manager what jobs I've applied for, I responded, 'An Australia Council Grant.' 'Good for you!' she exclaimed, as if the application itself was some sort of achievement. Enquiring about review work is less acceptable. I've never worked out why this is, but last month I won an unlikely concession: 'OK, we'll allow for one review.'

I'm a source of bafflement to DRAB. My right arm—my physical deficit—is easy to understand; not so the cognitive. I'm a writer but my first drafts are full of holes. I spell by sight rather than sound. I switch pronouns and participles. When such things are explained, I sense DRAB's incredulity. *You're a writer who can't spell? You teach English but you need to draft your emails?*

'You *sound* fine.'

The Affair
Shady Cosgrove

The plane ticket arrived during COVID—a long, thin envelope in the mailbox, my name printed on the outside. It was one of those old ones, departures and arrivals layered on top of each other in red and blue ink. But there was no travelling then—only chartered flights for stranded citizens. Had to be a joke.

Even so, I didn't tell anyone, kept it locked in my desk. The flight left in eight weeks and I didn't recognise the destination. I'd forget about it: my life was fine. But, of course, I wasn't sleeping then and after a couple of nights, I tiptoed to the study. Black sky gleamed outside, the window wet with rain. I slid key into drawer, checking the ticket was still there. Innocuous as a piece of paper. See—nothing, I told myself.

A month passed, and I was checking my desk three, four times a day. I'd stopped sleeping in my bed: instead, curling up in that high-backed leather chair.

4am, morning of the flight, and I caught the train. A change of clothes in my roller bag, a mask over my face, I sat alone at the back of the carriage. No one else on board. At the airport, the ticket counters were unmanned, shops dimmed—a ghost terminal. I moved through security, taking my laptop out of the bag, placing watch and belt in the requisite blue plastic tray, but I could have walked straight through.

Alone at the gate, I waited for my row to be called, and shuffled down the ramp. No stewards or stewardesses as I stepped on board, but I found my row, halfway along, and shifted over to the window seat. Seatbelt clicked into place, cabin eerie. The door closed and the plane pulled out. Empty. No voice from the captain.

The plane lifted and the seatbelt sign pinged. I stared through the plexiglass at the dark. If I know anything, I can say this with certainty: we flew in a straight line. The plane never dipped or angled. There was no turbulence. But when the aircraft landed, I disembarked at the same terminal I'd just left.

Back home, when I slid the key into my front door and kicked off my shoes, the house was quiet. I tiptoed from room to room, watching from each threshold—everyone was still sleeping.

Immigrant Allegiance
Shady Cosgrove

Middle of COVID and America wants feedback on her poems. The workshops start with messages and emails, sometimes live streaming: everything online. Sometimes days pass with no word. Maybe it's the time difference—she could be asleep now. Or maybe she's playing hard to get.

I'm lucky on this Antipodean island where no one has to wear a mask to the supermarket and we can afford to be slow with rolling out vaccinations until we can't. I shouldn't be looking elsewhere, but she remembers the island where I grew up. She's been drunk at KVI Beach, skinny dipping in the summer-cold Puget Sound. She's sat in my childhood kitchen, tripping on acid, while we spooned cookie dough onto baking trays.

I'm back in Sydney lockdown now, planes still grounded. America said we'd have a festival-reunion when I make it back—all of our friends, camping—but she's gone off the rails, ranting on social media, and we're no longer talking. I know she's sick, angry at herself maybe. My sister has a room waiting and I'm keeping an eye on flights, but memory is just fantasy and the ocean has never seemed so wide.

Wellington peonies
December 2020
Lynn Davidson

There are gushy peonies outside the florists' door.
Don't you just want to push your face into them? the florist says
which is a kindness because
I am already pushing my face into them.

So petalled. So inhabited. So pink. And
bunched together in a zinc bucket like something
cheaper, less luscious, more ordinary.

Mrs Dalloway said she would buy the flowers herself.
Netted by light and breathing rivery London air. Oh
to blossom into invisibility! To walk through the uncanny
narrow glade between buildings, that sudden temperature drop.
To see people in long coats at the bus stop undulate
in late spring wind, like kelp forests.

Bliss. Katherine Mansfield has Bertha arrange green and purple grapes
on a long, glossy table. Bertha is in a sudden ecstasy for a life
she is about to lose. Of course, she doesn't know it yet. She thinks only that
the purple grapes bring the carpet up to the table.

From Scotland to New Zealand
Lynn Davidson

I sit on the shore
recovering from this

long breath-held dive to get here.
The shudder of relief
to breathe in air.

Such air in this place .... the river of wind
Between   these islands
lands
here and   here and
here

Less breathing in

material

Less breathing in material.

How to measure land-loss against
the gentle constant of breath.

I have left Scotland—the word, the place—
the way we move through each other like light through water.

Infrastructure will not solve distance.
Nor can you build a country inside another country.

However—a word that sounds like a river of wind
between islands—*however*

the word *bridge*, its excavating consonants,
its failing reach,
sits deep in the gullies of my mouth.

a timid database
Dave Drayton

the sitter situates	a timid database
what walls absorb	of hearsay & witness
while the pages	and you pretend
go unfilled	gratuitously to be

capable of

omission

a mission

the violence that	they all would have
hung from gates	you believe
they could inflict	upon you while
dogs' mouths agape	seconding the threat

weep

whelp

settler, up thee accusations	settle up the hours
we asked you to create haste	honoured under eyes

because an acorn is both

that and it is a weapon

but only one will be a tree

cold feet
Dave Drayton

Mayfair

may fair well

for some but   not for others

it's not so easy   not all mothers

have a white Corolla

roll right past

the front gate to   yell in tongues

modify the timidity   of the air

but not the flight path of the fruit bats

or the clouds above the black cloud they are

or the flight paths of planes above

clouds both

a storm batters   boredom donning

crowded parkas   floodwater from

a broken dishwasher

comes to match the chill of the tiles

banish her

banister

leads to a story	the floor below
filled with primrose	will paraphrase
the toes lost	when doors were
upon cold feet	slammed shut

fingerprinted mucus stamps a postcard sent from an ex occupant

excess mustard also bruised the water

bill that enjoys equal pendency upon

the fridge held in place by the magnetic

calling cards of tradesmen and take-away

Chinese

Nightingale
Katrina Finlayson

There were murmurs of a revolution but I guess everyone was just too damn tired to do anything about it. In my home city in South Australia, we sheltered through a fairly short and relatively gentle lockdown. Sourdough starter, victory gardens, disinfecting delivery groceries on the front verandah, you know, and we are back on with life now. I mean, sure, there are now social distancing signs everywhere, and QR codes and registers, and you can't hug your friends at events if they are wearing a Covid Marshall fluoro vest, and you can get fined for dancing at a public event. Not quite the scale of change you'd expect from a global apocalypse.

The kid, barely two years old, doesn't know any other childhood. It's only me with unrealised ideas about what this time might be like. His playgroup even ran weekly videoconference sessions. Carefully concealing myself off-camera, I laughed seemingly endless tears at a Brady Bunch mosaic of toddlers running into the frame and away again, blurry faces suddenly looming too close to the camera, jerky movements as they danced the 'Wiggly Woo' together.

And yeah, we've been seeing constant streams of images of masked queues and sick people on the telly for the past year. And during isolation, I kept a keen eye on the daily state health department pressers on social media, for numbers of new and active cases. But soon enough, the new cases count dropped to zero. Border restrictions continue, yes, but the state death toll stopped at four many months ago.

Really, it's fine; we are fairly safe in our home and in our state and even in our country and the kid doesn't know any different. It's only me who is some days too anxious to sleep, to write, to leave the house.

'You better wash your hands, Mama,' he says, as we emerge together from a toilet cubicle at a Sunday outdoor market.

'Yes,' I say, 'you're right.'

Cute.

He thinks the crosses and circles 1.5 metres apart on the ground are dance spots, because that's what I told him. He jumps on each one: wiggle wiggle, wiggle wiggle. Giggle giggle.

Hah.

Although there was that one night when he half-woke suddenly, too many hours before dawn.

'I need to go to the dance spot,' he slurred through sleep and darkness.

He began to repeat it, like a chant, with growing urgency, as I quickly gathered his tiny body up and drew it close to mine.

'Sleep now, honeybee,' I murmured.

Surely, I reassured myself, these tiny bones know nothing about a year-long global pandemic. My sweet nightingale child.

Velkommen Hjem
Katrina Finlayson

Granted special permission to travel, a friend took a flight to Norway for her mother's funeral. When she returned a few months later, another friend made a roster of visitors to try and ward off the combined shock and depression of grief, jetlag, and two weeks of solo quarantine. We were to stand on the steps of Parliament House and wave to her in her hotel room directly across the road.

I consulted a translation site and made a huge cardboard sign for me and the tiny child to wave: *Velkommen Hjem*. We caught a train into the city. I called my friend on the phone to let her know we were there.

'I'll put some pants on,' she said.

One arm dangled awkwardly from a tiny open window so far above street level. I waved back and tried to point it out to the tiny child, but I'm pretty sure he was looking at a pedestrian crossing sign instead.

'What does the sign say?' my friend asked. 'I can't quite read it from here.'

I wrapped the sign around a package of home baked goods (gingerbread, brandy-soaked Christmas cake, shortbread) and secured it with a rubber band and we crossed the street and spoke briefly with a masked and sombre hotel entrance guard. I addressed the package with my friend's name and room number and added a love heart. I left the package on a desk just inside the front doors of the hotel. The foyer beyond the desk loomed dark and full of danger and we hurried away, back into the sunshine, to catch the next train home.

Centre Aisle
Laura Fulton

The alarm goes off too early but, with the end of daylight savings, 5:00am still feels like 6:00.

The dark of the new Melbourne morning is mild, this side of chilly, but my cardigan is enough. Sydney will be warm when the plane lands in a few hours from now.

The plane is small, but enough for this regional flight, two seats either side of the centre aisle in Business and Economy X, three in economy where we're headed. Every seat is full, and it seems odd sharing such tight quarters with so many strangers, despite the security of our snug masks.

I have not travelled since that day a year ago when reality shifted, March 24th, the day the first lockdown began in Melbourne, the day the kids came home from school, our borders shut, our doors closed, our world fell silent. On this, my inaugural flight in so long, I notice every single fellow passenger: the older man with shirt buttons straining against his pale white belly, the jaunty fellow in his jaunty hipster flat cap, the braw young guy in his tight t-shirt with the line of Hebrew script tattooed on the underside of his upper arm.

In a moment, I will marvel once again at the miracle of human flight, rise above the fairy floss clouds, feel for that moment when the apocalyptic roar of grinding engines and tiny tyres on runway suddenly shifts as we lift into the air.

But for now, I enjoy this simple pleasure: being surrounded by people, annoying and weird and wonderful, people I do not know.

beyond the dark line of trees
Jane Frank

we captured the stills of emptiness
swapped videos for paintings
souls somehow unswitched
a world of silent readers
in a *scriptio continua*
I suppose
if a page speaks at all
it is not silent
and the mystery of where roads take us
was dreams only buried in boxes
we walked towards them each day
across the lacustrine park
beyond the brick church buttressed
against a sky half pulled down
on a merse of memory
everything beyond
the dark line of trees
redacted

*

relief now to let words languish
in our mouths after the long
months of silent reading
feel the sting
of the elastic band bridge
fling us into the moss-covered suburbs
with their shiny obsidian roads
beneath dust, slow electrum light
glinting down from the sleepy mountain
we are denizens of the north
allowed back

Poem for the End of Time
Stephanie Green

The Pacific rises and the city lights go out. Against a wafting sky, glass towers reflect fractals of despair. Cats prowl the roofs, lashing their tails and batting at clouds with jagged paws. Vermin dredge the drains for quiet survival. Like us, there are too many of them now. Keep walking.

At midnight the Nasdaq falls and the rest follow in grim relay. The last of the oil is too deep to tap. Sorghum is scarce. Graders have scraped fertility from the soil. Life is measured in hungry children and the weight of sand. Keep walking.

Migrant birds fan out above, searching for where the last fringes of forest hold sway. We tell ourselves the war is somewhere else. Some area to the north or the east we can't name. There's no seeing up ahead. Follow the birds. They, if anything, might show us what we've lost. Keep walking.

Beyond the city, the last red coals are dying. Eddies of white ash rise with each foot fall. Smoke hangs on the windless air. We hardly notice the crunch of skeletons. It's the incessance that's hardest to bear. If only it were over. If only we could rest. Keep walking. They don't want us here. Keep walking.

Rust
Stephanie Green

In the kitchen my father ate his lunch every day after my mother died, salads, tinned fish, brown bread. An old man tapping his left toe in time with the refrigerator's hum. As he worked in his shed, he'd whistle a show tune he'd heard as a child, on the phonograph that was burned with the stamp album and box brownie photographs, in the great fire of memories when my grandfather lost his mind. Under the house was a metal hat box where the old papers were kept, a rusted bed frame and a black bakelite telephone that long ago lost its connection. All that's left now are his stories of walking over a bed of snakes on a scented tropical night, and foggy winter mornings when he couldn't see to drive, hands buttoned into wool-lined leather gloves, gripping the steering wheel as he tried to see the way ahead. I rest a photograph of him in an old metal frame on the shelf above my desk, taken before I was born, so I can say hello to him sometimes, on foggy mornings, or summer evenings after sunset.

Refuge
Rebecca Hamilton

The street was dark when they arrived. Liam guessed at least another two streetlights had blown since their last stay. He parked across a pothole and turned to his mother, sprawled in the passenger seat. He didn't yet have his licence—wasn't even old enough for a learner's permit—but when he'd seen the tremor in his mother's hands and the glaze in her eye, he'd had no choice.

Turning off the engine, Liam pulled a pack of cigarettes from the centre console and a lighter from his pocket. When his mother jolted awake, he slipped them down the side of his seat.

'What time is it?'

'Almost ten.'

She rubbed her eyes and Liam thought fast. He opened the console again and, with a sleight of hand, produced the cigarettes. She lit up right away, and he made a show of batting away the smoke curling towards his face.

'Sorry, love.' She wiped her glistening forehead. 'I know I should quit.'

He folded his lips together and tucked them aside. 'Yeah, well. One thing at a time.'

The grey building seemed smaller, but Liam knew it was a mind-trick, the world shrunk by the growth spurt that had stretched his skin like cling film, leaving silken stripes across his broadening back and shoulders. But other changes were real. The bindi-infested grass had gone, and the old brick path had been replaced with shiny new pavers.

When they reached the door, Liam pressed the buzzer. He hoped to hear a familiar voice. Doubted it would be a new one on the night shift; it was against policy. Unless the policy had changed, of course, like he had. He glanced down at his rubber-thonged feet, then up at the doorframe with which he now stood at eye level. He rubbed his neck at the thought of the low ceilings.

The intercom croaked to life, and a tiny beam of light illuminated a small camera. He stood aside and let his mum do the talking. They were back.

Rain
Thomas Hamlyn-Harris

R's hands mirror each other on the steering wheel in the ten and two positions. She has pulled into the emergency lane on the Bruce Highway.

'It's only a few drops of rain,' I say.

'I know, I just need a minute.'

Despite these moments of panic, I love teaching my daughter to drive. This is her first time driving in the rain. I begin to explain the windshield wipers. The rain gets heavier and she's not listening. I watch her hands, still in the ten and two positions, and notice the small white scar on the side of her left hand.

R was born blue with six fingers on her left hand. I got to hold her briefly, bloodily before she was taken by the nurse. A red button on the wall was pushed. I expected to be surrounded by lab coats while delicate procedures were explained in hushed tones. But when I saw R again her hand was bandaged and she was a healthy, screaming pink. Nothing was noted on the chart, so I assumed this kind of thing happened all the time.

Now I question if R really had an extra finger or if it was something I dreamed or conjured. I think about the witches or elves or celestial patterns that would have been blamed if she had been born in another time. Would she have been left for dead in a dry creek bed? Stoned to death? Or worshipped as a benevolent chimerical Goddess?

Her phantom little finger is positioned perfectly to adjust the windshield wipers. I contemplate telling R. Will she feel incomplete, like a piano with a missing minor key? A truck whooshes past and the car rocks gently.

'Can you drive?' she asks, releasing her grip from the wheel and holding her hands together in her lap.

'Nah,' I say. 'Let's just sit here until the rain passes.'

Π
Dominique Hecq

A whiff of butter, caramel, French fries and booze in the air that swells in this city's cooing clamour. Voiceless, you follow your feet. Up and up they climb the bumpy cobbled streets toward a medieval castle's remains. All around, the walls of the old town radiate heat. Up they walk you, your feet, to the tipping point of the landscape. They take you to Villa Noailles. Closing time. You sit down on a garden bench. Your parched skin soaks in stray droplets of water from the sprinklers. You wonder what time they close the gate. Notice the height of the iron fence.

She arrives the way birds do. Soundlessly. Fleetingly. Drinking the air. Irony in her gaze. She perches next to you. Unties your tongue: π, you say, don't mind me I'm only gathering fragments of living.

Π laughs. Asks if you've been to the salt marshes on the Giens peninsula. Says she loves waterbirds. That you should go to Porquerolles; walk the rocky trails and snorkel in the *criques* for they are full of underwater shipwrecks. This would suit you, who inhabits no space, but time's broken line.

Vous n'êtes pas très loquace, says π in this strange tongue full of understatements, reiterations, reproaches, this plu-perfect tongue that once allowed you to renounce what may have been.

It's November, or June. *Hier*. Her name is Prose or Rose. Avid. And I, emptying. Already empty. *Vide*. How words climb back time and give way to what can only be encountered step by step.

Words shot with odours of butter and caramel, echoes, sensations. Melting moments. And now this bird woman with a tongue sharp as a blade who converses silently with magpies in the brokenness of time. Elusive.

Hyères, between dog and wolf. Anything could happen.

like so many turns of phrase on the narrow and pebbly road one burns bridges cross broken bridges woken bridges before the awakening of dreams without borders before the language of words with its gaps misprints bricolages and reverberating echoes and one says nothing and let all slip by out of daylight past palm trees defying the very notion of gravity yes past

(…)

the night, with its engulfing mouth, is scarier than the velvet sea when a wild boar appears in a shroud of mist and blackbirds gobble up summer's purple solitude and loneliness and rage dissipate into rhythms of mortal light

Notes

Vous n'êtes pas très loquace: you don't talk much, do you?

Hyères is a real town in the South of France that rhymes with *hier* (yesterday).

Vigil
Dominique Hecq

Night, laced with mist,

    a slight quiver of breeze, oblivious

to the internal weather of your heart,

    you watch your brilliant window recast
in full reflection the white linen curtains billowing
                  gently.

Here, heeere, calls a currawong, and you are back at the water's edge, watching
a plastic bag bobbing along the creek, or some severed head smooth as the moon.

You taste the bitter taste of juniper, inhale the damp
reek of a body cleaved from a bed of reeds and roots, all
                                entangled.

Nothing holds it now, the body. It balloons downstream, leaving
                              you unleaving.

                      Sweat on your thinning skin evaporates, or is it silt
                      dusting its translucence as your Dante holds vigil
                          at the sinking moon, and you sur
                                                  f
                                                  a
                                                  c
                                                  e

You forget where you are; everything is

cold to the touch.

Wavelets unfold before you, voice a trickle of white ink.

City
Paul Hetherington

We intended to stay for a week in this untidy city. Now most days we play games in the amusement arcade or walk on the pebble beach in front of the famous colonial-era hotel. You paint pictures of nineteenth-century buildings in delicate dabs of watercolour, and we swim in the lagoon's shallows not far from tourists in their white-tiled pool. I read novels or write long emails. In the afternoon we drink short blacks or fanciful cocktails. Before long you say you're getting used to the place, pointing to an advertisement for a rental apartment. A year passes and you look for a place to buy. I remind you that we intended to go to Venice, but you say we are not those people, waving my remark away. You hand me a glass of Pinot Noir: 'Of course, we are here.'

Tunnel
Paul Hetherington

There are closed windows and doors in the mall. Announcements on the news refer to the end of the 'normal'. Sand gusts remind you of a beach where you slid into a tunnel your schoolfriend had dug—where you lay as wind gathered force and she put her hand on your leg. She told you a risqué story and laughed. You imagine the vista of that beach, remembering the saltiness of her skin—and entertain an idea of the past as simultaneously insufficient and marvellous—as a grappling wind pushes you into a café. An old acquaintance is working there and asks what you want, but you cannot tell him. You see yourself turning away, nodding, saying you'll catch up soon, feeling the palpable address of fingers.

A chart of the incompleteness of human experience, one year on, as described by C Howe in the year 2021

Christine Howe

2020-2021	DISCARDED	COVETED	FINDINGS	DIRECTIONS
CONCEPTS	Certainty.	According to moss and lichen,	I am often wrong.	There is no clear path through
LIVING THINGS	Swathes of waist-long hair (snipped short by a nine-year-old), carefully selected by a nesting magpie.	I crave time with people I love;	I have learned that living with animals awakens gentleness and curiosity—as does	living in community, like trees do.
LIFE MATTERS	Piles of unopened superannuation statements;	mashed potato and butter;	paying attention in the garden.	Community is messy. It is made up of effort and misunder-standings. Community is sitting in a crowded theatre, hoping no-one coughs. It is
BOOKS	Julia Baird's *Phosphorescence* (the second half);	Kate Liston-Mills' *Dear Ibis* (all of it);	Robin Wall Kimmerer's *Braiding Sweetgrass* (speaks of reciprocal relationships between people, plants and animals);	Joshua Lobb's *Flight of Birds* (adapted into *Fledgling*, a play by Lily Hayman. Feel the energy of the actors, marvel at the props. Smell the stage smoke,
NOURISH-MENT	and tooth decay.	Iced VoVos (my granny's favourite); and cups of tea.	I feel the injustice of my plenty in the face of others' need	and sense an audience breathing).

The Last Time We Saw Each Other
Anita Jawary

Under the shade of grape vines, we sit side by side in the courtyard of a nursing home that slumps, like an afterthought, behind the hospital.

Mum, look!

I point you to the mint and parsley growing in small wooden boxes ahead of us, avoiding your smile—pitted teeth, yellow-black. Your hazel eyes, once speckled with laughter, now glassy with medication.

I point.

You nod.

Two women rich in words, well practised at silence, we tucked our words into the zipped compartments of our purses long ago and can't get the zips unstuck.

I watch your fingers, knobbled and useless in your lap—once so busy with knitting needles, you would twist the wool to strangulation. I want to strangle you, I want to love you.

Those who say that understanding brings forgiveness are wrong.

The coinage we hoarded so long is out of date. All we have now, on this last day under the grapevine, are pins of light and cooling shade, gifts from a tangled vine.

But we did see each other one more time, by the sea you loved so much.

You flew towards me, your wings wide and white against a bright blue sky.

O, beautiful gull! You hovered for what seemed an eternity on the buoyant wind, holding my gaze with your small, black-gull eyes.

In that lingering look, you bound me with all the love you'd struggled so long to unravel, and with an apology, for all the debris you'd left behind.

Toxic Towers
Sue Joseph and Anon

```
        TOXIC   TOWERS
      ┌─────────────────────┐
      │      OBSTRUCT       │
      │    REVENGEINAD      │
      │    EQUACYVIOLE      │
      │    NCEINEPTITU      │
      │    DESTRESSINT      │
      │    IMIDATIONSA      │
      │    DISTICBULLYR     │
      │    EPULSIONDIS      │
      │    ENFRANCHISE      │
      │    DPALPITATIO      │
      │    NSRETREATAT      │
      │    TACKHATREDD      │
      │    ENIALEGOSBI      │
      │    LESOCIOPATH      │
      │    YGRIEFPSYCH      │
      │    OPATHYTEARS      │
      │    ANXIETYHIDEU     │
      │    NDERMINING       │
      │    WHITEANTING      │
      │      GOODBYE        │
      └─────────────────────┘
```

Spent Ink
Daniel Juckes

> *I am writing all this down in blue ink, so as to remember that all words, not just some, are written in water.*
>
> Maggie Nelson, Bluets, 92

I make the effort to put them in order: from the thin and clear, stretching towards those more dregs-laden, and even seeming-full of deepest blue. Then the line they track becomes a wash of white fading to its opposite. But close in there are errors in the map they make of colour. And even in the photographs I take of my experiment—of those parts of the chain which seem to work best—there is evidence of disorder.

I keep them in a plastic container. Inside, they rattle like rain—or, like the sound of rain made from peas and pebbles turned upside-down through the hollow body of a dried-out cactus. So perhaps, instead, they sound like rain explained.

There are 149 of them. There would be more, if I had been more careful: I left, for instance, a pile behind—in England—after writing there. Occasionally, too, they fall in gaps or find themselves rolling on or blown away: when the ink which was inside them dries they are light, and as they go they turn a curved path, an irregular parabola set by how much residue remains—as well as, of course, by their shape and by the weight of the miniature widget each contains. I choose a cartridge, cut into its heart, and see what that small thing feels like. It is hard and almost painful to squeeze, and leaves a faint sphere on my thumb-tip after it falls, with Lilliputian clatter, onto kitchen tiles to once more hint at rain.

Altogether, in line, they measure exactly a metre—the cartridges themselves, that is. I do not know how long the trail their spent content adds up to, nor can I map the shapes or blots they have made across my hands: I am forever finger-stained. It is, of course, unclear why I keep them—unless the thing I crave most is the sense of permanence they promise, despite the sense of promise they permanently resist. There is always the idea of what they might bring coupled with the whisper of what they have brought; all the half-plottings and mixed shapes they have helped and hindered in the telling.

Wings
Helena Kadmos

COVID writes new poetry with our bodies. Hands that would reach forward, hesitate, and retreat. Moves to embrace are questions that dissolve into shrugs, embarrassed chuckles, elbow kisses. But touch is a memory with a long shadow.

While the community grappled with what it meant to live with disease, learning to go inward, recede from all but necessary physical contact, my family was asked to open wide and make room for someone else—a child who needed a home. Every Friday our bodies resurrected routines we'd thought were behind us: steering the car into a kiss-and-drive, shoving a back-pack between knees, turning a too-bright face toward a blank stare, asking, how was school today? Then, a weekend of snack-making, room-tidying, ball-catching, dance-steps watching, close-the-door reminding, Band-Aid-applying, shower-nagging, book-reading, good-night-kissing. Feeling old. Feeling unsure. Wondering ... what touch is too much? How much does she need? How much can I give?

Getting it right. She, overcome by rare equanimity on my part, nestled under my armpit, curled over her own balled-fists. Me—wise enough to keep my mouth shut for once.

Getting it wrong. Me—too hurried, getting cross. She—flinching and freezing. Me—wringing uncertain hands. Between us, a ravine.

Spring, summer, autumn. The end arrives sooner than we expected. We are thanked for what we did but we don't feel enlarged. There's been no obvious breakthrough, no light-cracking realisation. Just, easing ... out ... and back.

I'm in her home. Not the home we shared, the one she's returned to. She scoots across the mattress to invite me in. Eight months since she came to us, and she's grown a lot, but I pretend I can easily fit. She faces the wall, trying to hide from me the stuffed toy she's shoved under her pillow. I fold my arm, like a wing, over hers so that our tips meet, and stroke her fingers, trying to still them. She asks me if I like the starry lights strung along the bed-head. I say they are very pretty.

I rub her back, but can tell I won't loosen the tightness at her core.

I say goodnight, and that I'll see her in a few weeks. But we've just come out of one snap lockdown, and I don't know if my promise is true.

Maybe this moment will last for us both.

To Mauritius
Dean Kerrison

Together you stare at the stars, waves collapsing, she laments a year passing, how nothing's changed, a deadlock, and if you knew today was fourteen nanoseconds longer than this day was a year ago you'd tell her, but you study the lazy half-moon, saying *I know, I wanna sail to Mauritius, at least illness aboard in the great big blue is predictable,* unaware the moon has travelled in the past twelve months, further from Earth now, so you take a day trip together on a boat with speed bumps splashing sparkling wine from plastic flutes, and she points out a boy laughing, running side to side across the deck, but bliss is coated only on the bottom half of her face, shady sunnies hiding the rest, and you're unsure how she feels losing a year of fertility and her man who was meant to be here but now he's somewhere within the stars, an Indian Ocean droplet down her cheek and she drops the flute, sweat lining your face, off the speeding boat you dive, snorkel set on with Mauritius in sight, legs fatiguing, plummeting to the sand beyond the reach of the full moon's glow cast across the surface.

Childhood Dreaming
Jeri Kroll

Woke up once more adrift in the past, wondering if I'll dream the future again. All my son's childhood ingrained in the stones and timber of our razed Federation house. Measuring him against the mantelpiece became a ritual, as necessary as communion for a Catholic, making me worthy of the Order of Mothers. On the peeling white paint, this last message in permanent marker: 'We couldn't fit him under.'

Another image preserved for the future, his toddler handprint in clay. I run my finger along its grooves, whisper the rhyme on the back, the words open a wormhole to 1989.

A brilliant morning sun filters through leadlight, staining my legs blue-green, as I lift his immortal hand from the bookcase. I'm forty-three, wondering how I'll feel a decade on. He would be a teen, my own body resisting middle-age. Even now the future collects like dust on the skirting.

That year marks our first lockdown too. As soon as I notice baubles glisten on his shoulder, I know he has chickenpox. We are due at his grandmother's for Christmas, but cannot go now. She's had leukemia and is 'vulnerable', a word that has evolved like a virus.

And yet that holiday lingers in my memory. The weather is Goldilocks perfect, the neighbourhood hushed, only snatches of music or conversation float in the air.

While my son sprawls on the couch, mesmerized by the TV, his father putters in the garden and I go for a run. When I pelt in through the gate, a glorious scent lures me to the bronzed turkey resting in the kitchen. What an odd way to describe a bird that will never need a nap again. I scratch off a flap of crispy skin before heading to sort my son's clothes.

All in all, it's a golden day, light flushed like freshly baked pastry, filled with the serene whistling of birds, the murmur of cats, the dog's nails on veranda tiles, even the babble of the TV.

I've kept the images of that Christmas quarantined as if I'd stored them in a locket. I open it now and become that woman of forty-three kneeling on a scratchy carpet, wondering if I dare tempt fate and keep these outgrown clothes for a possible future. I take that locket on its chain decades-long and hang it over my heart.

Explorer on the Moon: 2021
Joshua Lobb

I'm not Tintin. Orbiting the moon in my chunky orange space suit, a deep-sea diver in the ocean of space, spinning into an infinity of adventures, fearlessly flying into deepest darkest wherever: wild west America, Stalinist Russia, the tangled jungles of the Amazon. And now the moon. I remember the picture from the book: a full page of the craterous expanse, the black empty sky. A speck of a figure. *This is it!* he cries. *I've walked a few steps! For the first time in history, there is an EXPLORER ON THE MOON!* The gravity is lighter there. Your head spins. Captain Haddock would rather stay in the cigar-cocoon of the rocket, but grudgingly clambers down to the grey sand. Tintin and the captain head off in their lunar tank across the lumpy surface. They follow a groove on the surface; it splits into a narrow valley, worn down by an infinity of moondust. The captain spots a crack in the valley wall, an opening to a new adventure, a cave. Tintin and Snowy venture out in their orange deep-sea space suits. Snowy strides ahead and falls deeper into a crevasse. Tintin follows. As he drops into the unknown he cries, *Into the hands of fate!*

I'm not Tintin. Not even Captain Haddock, refusing the adventure, but grudgingly going anyway. The gravity is heavier here. Headier. Under the rumples of the duvet, hiding from deepest darkest everything. Nothing ventured. Trying to work up the courage to open the door and face the dusty air, to step into a yellow-lit supermarket, to climb into the cigar-cocoon of a bus again. The lumps of crowds, the ocean of bodies. My narrow strip of life round the block, an adventure of one foot in front of the other. Avoiding confrontations with breathing human faces. The tightness of fear. Tangled up in the orange and purple darkness of my own spinning brain. Avoiding all hands at all costs.

Year of Breath
December 31, 2020
Rose Lucas

All this long year
        its cramps of anxiety
      its rolling replications and blows of
grief   blows to the temple   or

the building of its quiet routines while
we all stayed home   and step
by stumbling step   found different
ways to think about our lives

all this strange year   the battered world
has kept on   breathing   even
as we see   writ large
the fragility

      the sometime-ness
of this respiring machine   the always risk of
catch   choke of tightness
the certain knowledge   that the small currents

of this   one body   will one day
    falter   breath hole empty
washed away in other   widening tides

The Weather Up Here
Mia Francesca Michelle McAuslan

Summer in the bush—at first I thought, too hot, too boring and dry. Instead, it moved me. The black cows against the blonde grass, the bird calls bright and clear like morning.

Then, last year, my brother's first baby was due. I was grieving his becoming. The borders were closed and I knew I couldn't be there. During this time the 1890s miners' cottage—with its heritage frontage, original wood stove, birds nesting in the chimney—was riddled with ghosts. I walked down the long hallway in the dark night with intention, the same way my mother taught me to walk past a horse or a man, or anything that might menace you if it senses fear.

At Easter, the baby comes to visit. Now that he is here, the house doesn't feel so big and I'm less afraid. We walk through the grassy field that used to be a gold mine. When we stop, he pulls himself up onto the charcoal stump of a burnt down tree. I offer my leg to steady him.

In this moment, I realise that he is already making memories—the sun reflecting on my red boot, my white ankle, and the crisp husk of the stump.

Rattus and Oxen
Gay Lynch

Rats darken deserted restaurant doorways, the pandemic year. I howl at heart-shadows during aerobic exercise and family-skypes about Mother's dying. And during orgasms—those domestic little deaths. Mostly I am mute. Write as if I am dying, under lockdowns and slatey skies.

I run, heavy with dread. Kick-box. Wait. Trapped within state borders. Then without. Read obsessively into the night. We sisters rush into hotel quarantine, live monk-like on brown rice and canned corn, until we blitz four Covid swabs, to reach our mother's bedside.

'Poor little buggers,' she says, 'stuck in a room for a fortnight, even with their stupid computers.'

Trapped like rats behind wainscot.

A godly man, ponytailed, gifts Mother a wooden cross. Perhaps she'd prefer, a crossword.

'Put on my rings,' she commands. 'I want to sleep and never wake up.'

Follows her bagpiping brother to the last space in the swamp.

'I sleep on the left,' she says, 'my husband on the right.' But they have sold Father's plot. Will she move over for him?

The year of the Ox supplants the Rat and on we plod like Grandfather's team, an uncertain future until, briefly, on trams, their windows flung wide, we seek the city again to borrow a bagful of books at the Ballieu. An historian and I mask up @ Paperback Bookshop and Pellegrinis. Sink a bottle at Bottegas, beneath plane trees.

Oxygen runs out on sub-continents. Covid mutates. Four months on, my father fails to thrive.

'I made a mistake staying behind,' he mourns. Medicos push him off a morphine cliff. I time his breathing, stroke his mottled hand. Cheyne-stoke breaths rattle and grind at the back of his throat. Ten-second stops, whistles. Vitality oozes yellow from his lips. Whatever made him original has fled. Annulled his forthcoming birthday.

Father relinquishes command in the Aethereum. Indeed, a *woman* drives his hearse.

Careless to lose two parents, we joke. I wear a black eye to his funeral.

CIB nephew peers into my face. 'I've written it up,' he says.

'Get an AVO on *moi*,' I say. 'Muay Thai. Punched myself in the head.'

Papa's little peeps lean into the grave to scatter potpourri. Rain shines in their hair. One hunkers down with her pink umbrella, shakes her red feathered-Follies head-dress over the hole.

'What's going on?' another asks. 'Everyone's dying.'

Cockatoos soar overhead, dark shapes in the paltry light. Scarcely a murmuration.

The Art of Letting Go
Mario Daniel Martín

> *To renounce things is not to give them up.*
> *It is to acknowledge that all things go away.*
>
> Shunryu Susuki Roshi

When I was in my mid-twenties, through reading, I discovered Zen Buddhism. And because of these spiritual coincidences in life, learnt that in a small town, near the city where I lived, there was a sangha. I got involved and attended weekend sheshins, and later, eight-day retreats, in which people sat in meditation all day facing a wall, concentrating on koans, illogical questions that force Zen students to go beyond their habitual ways of thinking and respond with their deeper intuitive being. As a beginner, I was assigned mu, which originally means simply 'not'.

The flashes of insight, however, did not happen in these retreats, but in unexpected places. Doing the dishes, waiting for a green light when driving, licking ice cream in the city square, sitting on a bench in front of the baroque cathedral.

When I left the city, and then my country, I carried with me the habit of meditating. Even ten or fifteen minutes of pounding through mu in the morning, before facing the day ahead, made a big difference. It helped me survive my PhD, my initiation into the rat race of academia, and throughout the earthquake of becoming a father. However, I was a lonely wolf, meditating on my own, as the energies were put into the outside world.

During a sabbatical semester, before the pandemic, I began attending mindfulness classes, which included a one-day silent meditation retreat. The meditation training did not emphasise koans, but shikantaza, the practice of choiceless awareness, following your breath, allowing everything that occurs inside or outside you to pass through, without focussing on it. Sitting again in meditation for several hours, pulling myself back, over and over to the experience of the moment, I was visited too often by the academic world. As I sat watching my thoughts come and go, I realised that my life needed to change.

The pandemic madness struck, and I decided to use the time that I saved from commuting to work sitting in meditation. Eventually, I returned to explore koans, a different one each week.

The koan I was meditating with when the offer of a voluntary redundancy package came was 'standing atop a hundred-foot pole, take a step forward'.

Against Entropy
Sam Meekings

i) Entropy, history of: beginning with the observation that in combustion reactions, a little functional energy is always lost and can therefore never turn into useful work.

[*Useful work* is a term used to describe a thermodynamic principle. Last night I slept, for once, untroubled by either insomnia or those strange and hopeless dreams in which the past ebbs further and further from my reach. As I throw open the curtains in the morning, my eyes are drawn to the fringes of the garden, to the elm-shaded nook that the early morning sunlight cannot reach. A squirrel, I think. Moving towards the tree. Up early and intent on his mission. This is useful work. I watch him for several hours.]

ii) Entropy, in information transmission systems: the comparable inevitability of missing information, or the data that is inevitably lost in each transmission.

[The squirrel stays so still that it seems as if he has stopped time through some immense act of willpower alone. Then he blinks, twitches, leaps along. Information gets lost in any system. If the squirrel could speak, he would say soon, soon, soon. The little gaps that open up between a word and its meaning. Soon, I would ask him. Soon? There is no longer any soon.]

iii) Entropy, in business metaphor: waste, inefficiency, the fat that might be trimmed if all teams are to maximise productivity.

[The squirrel has disappeared now. Slipped away at the end of the garden. As a kid I'd understood, instinctively, that if I made my way to the bottom of the garden I might find any number of strange and unexpected creatures that normally remain invisible. Fairies, sprites, goblins. Mr Tumnus, witches, a spare Tardis. One day soon I will go down to the bottom of the garden and find a pathway through to somewhere new. Maybe later. After I tick off today's to-do list.]

i) Entropy, colloquial: a sense of energy wasted or dissipated; breakup, degeneration; the gradual movement towards collapse or decline.

[Last night I slept in dribs and drabs, or at least drifted some. First thing I do in the morning is yank back the curtain, and there he is. That fluff-tailed scurry between the branches. A line of movement. A little good work. As if to say that nothing is wasted. The smallness of things. Distant possibilities. Enough to keep going.]

MURRAY'S COVIDICTIONARY:
more new words for testing times
Peta Murray

Artfoolness ▶ adjective
Mucking around in unschoolful ways in the ruins of the cloisterfuck

Bruize ▶ noun
Hip colour of the Anthropocoronacene applicable to skies, skin, hearts and hopes

Covidamnesia ▶ noun
Collective agreement to forget the paindemic

Drolling ▶ verb
Posting funny words online as a practice of ground-dogging

Euphorelia ▶ noun
Mix of glee, legumebriousness and anxiety felt in company of real people in real life in all their hectic embodiment

Fomophilia ▶ noun
A newfound joy in missing out

Guestervessence[1] ▶ noun
A fizzy burst of energy before a reunion with a beloved bubbler

Horrorscoping ▶ noun
Inability to see anything but gloom, virtigo and disaster in one's future

Isoscope ▶ noun
Any device (including a quarantini) that gives a glimpse of the absurdity and insignificance of one's existence

Junefulness ▶ adjective
An eruption of song somewhere near midwinter through which online choirs spread kroonervirus

Kohlerabies ▶ noun
Virally-transmitted images of Alan Kohler's bookstack (with vegetation) on The Finance Report delivered Moanday to Blursday on ABC News

Lullabide ▶ noun
An interval of quiet in which to settle into a nunnified detente with the world

Masketcase ▶ noun
A person who has arrived at a degree of masked mirth while telecarousing that renders communication impossible

Normswanclature ▶ noun
Re-naming things based on coronacastings from Guru physician and journalist Dr Norman Swan

Oneiroscapades ▶ noun
Bizarre adventures experienced in one's dreamscape, at the expense of one's youthage

Paria(h)dise ▶ noun
Entrumpy when one's home state is shut off from the rest of the nation

Qubbler[2] ▶ noun
The queer friend who joins you in your bubble for rehumanising

Ronageist ▶ noun
The defining spirit of a period of history as sculptured by the most virulent virus of its times

Solacious ▶ adjective
The power of sunshine to console and restore after pellage

Thymetravel ▶ noun
The olfactory potency of herbs, grasses and vegetation to transport one while in salutary confinement

Unwine ▶ noun
A relaxing beverage always consumed uncabinated

Videoduity ▶ noun
Bereavement following a zubarustistabundant binge on all twelve seasons of one's favourite TV show

Wistferia ▶ noun
Longing for lockdown as others start making xkerbitions of themselves

X-position ▶ noun
_____ (your word marks this spot)

Yulebrimmer ▶ noun
A seasonal reveller seeing out the old year from the comfort of their isobar

Zmorganiser[3] **▶ noun**
Person designated to curate online events in celebration of wideberthdays and other holidaze.

---

[1] Courtesy of R Burke

[2] Word courtesy of A Campbell & M Cohen

[3] Word courtesy of J Horacek

Two more weeks
Lili Pâquet

It's July; the air has a bite that promises snow. You wear your facemask, the navy blue one with paisley patterns that you bought from Etsy, with a nose wire to stop it fogging your glasses. You waddle from two blocks away, your thirty-eight-week belly stretching out in front of you like a smuggled basketball. Your pelvis splits apart with each step to the entrance. Hand sanitizer on your chapped hands.

'Appointment?'

'Mm,' you grunt and nod, voice croaky with disuse. The nurse beeps a thermometer at your forehead and sticks a pink dot on you.

You walk toward the obstetrician's office. He is an older gentleman with an Eastern European accent. He doesn't have a computer in his office, but instead looks you in the eyes when you talk and writes notes down in neat cursive. You are creeped out that this man will cut you open, like Jack the Ripper.

But today you go downstairs to the oncology department. You sit in the waiting room with a man who is impossibly thin and pale. You're embarrassed about the length of your hair, aided by COVID restrictions and pregnancy hormones. The cheery yellow walls, covered in pamphlets, make you squint.

You are ushered to a recliner, an IV drip inserted into your arm, iron pumped directly into your veins. The needle is cold, but the nurse places a warmed heat pack over top. You pull out a book but can't focus. People in the room look bored. One woman is there with a friend, laughing and drinking a takeaway coffee. Another nurse offers an egg salad sandwich on white bread. You are adrift and disconnected.

You rub your belly and imagine two weeks ahead. You conjure yourself on the couch at home, surrounded by McDonalds thickshakes. You've craved them since the day you saw a police officer drinking one. Your mouth salivates at the memory.

You expect a repeat of your last birth experience, but it won't be. This time around you won't struggle with depression and ignorance and blood-loss, and you'll enjoy your sleepy newborn with her fuzzy, scented head. You don't know this yet, all you know is that you really want a chocolate thickshake.

Pruning
Mary Pomfret

Three days and three rosaries it takes me to find the strength to open your letter. Exaggeration to call it a letter. A note would be a far more accurate description—you say it's best that we don't see each other again.

Days pass. Weeks. Months. I think of nothing but you. I hear your mother died, so I send my condolences. A card. I try so hard to be imaginative, memorable, but in the end I am generic: *So very sorry for your loss.*

You respond with a text message. *Thank you for your condolences.*

Enough. I must see you.

I take three poems I have written for you and a rock, carved in the shape of a face. The one we found, together.

I pull up outside your house and there you are, wearing your Akubra hat, pruning the roses in the blazing January sun.

Your eyes, steel blue, meet mine.

I begin my soliloquy. *I wish… I'm so sorry… maybe we could…*

You take my offerings and put them down by your front doorstep. You never use your front door and I wonder now if my sorrowful gifts are still there, with the rock on top, covered in dust and fallen leaves.

I hold out my hand and you shake it, hard, as if I am a man. I wish you well, you say, like an employer farewelling a staff member. I retreat down the garden path and stop at the blue wheelbarrow full of rosehips. I reach in and pluck out a cutting.

Put it back, you say, yelling.

But why?

Because it's DEAD.

But it's beautiful, I say, dropping the thorny twig back into the wheelbarrow.

You return to the task, cutting and discarding the misshapen rosehips.

Inkling
Mary Pomfret

Today, at the back of a dusty drawer, I find the heart-shaped birthday card I was going to send you last year. As I begin to write a salutation I recall the dishwashing scene—when you offered to help Juliette.

It was a long hot weekend—the first time you and I had been away on a camping trip in years.

A reasonable observer would no doubt think you were a sweet man, assisting a tired woman whose husband had been drinking shiraz all day in the sun. But I am not a reasonable observer. You, my long-time husband, had *never* offered to help me with the dishes. For Juliette, you picked up the tea towel as if it were a blessed altar cloth and wiped her glasses like a priest might polish a communion chalice.

I watched you both, your heads bent close together.

To send a greeting now would seem beyond foolishness, but I have already scratched your name in sharp black letters, and I never could abide waste.

Firesky
Julia Prendergast

We run, weaving between ironbark gums in early evening. The amber sky is misleading.

It's cold. We talk despite our foggy breathlessness.

So suddenly dark, you say.

Don't start with the solstice. I know your spiel by heart—the shortest day of the year—the day of least daylight—the darkest day.

The sun as north as north can be, you say, as if we're stuck on loop, as if a year hasn't passed—the same fern gully and clay tracks, bark and moss layered like a juxtaposition.

Some places have festivals, you say. *For death and rebirth.*

I spit into the wildgrass.

Another month before we reach the peak of coldness, you add. *A month after solstice—*

Please shut up, I say.

You blast the running app, marking our lap time.

Shut it off, I beg.

I hate the running app. Who cares how our form compares to yesterday, ten minutes ago, last month?

Why are we so afraid of the dark, *I mean* the silence …

The next day we run early in the hope that things feel new. When we reach the deepest part of the gully, there's no sign of Melbourne suburbia. Wet earth, brittle bark, spiralling birdcall—time in yesterdays.

Clear dew shines purple in the morning light—spindly green leaves, glittering with purple crystals.

I stop, reaching toward it. Against my fingertips it's cold water.

You, too, have stopped.

No sign of rain, I say. *How is it possible …? But don't answer. It's rhetorical.*

There's more energy escaping from the earth than being absorbed by the sun. Do you mean entropy is rhetorical?

Purple, I say.

My calf spasms. I shift to the closest tree. *Our* tree. I arch my underfoot against the exposed roots, glistening like sweaty thighs.

Six months ago, we lay here like teenagers, a blowjob in the summer dusk because what was the world coming to?

Treetops clawing like hungry fingers. Firesky.

Now the days grow shorter, over and again.

Self-flagellation and the Falls
Peter Ramm

> *Most of me is halfway here;*
> *the rest stands Halfway back and watches.*
>
> Mark Tredinnick

Mid-December, the day hardly awake

    In a semi-drizzle, the sun labouring

Hard to lose the weight of clouds. I walk

        In myself and out on the East Rim track

—A cicada a cappella showers

From the silvertops and I'm caught between calls

Of a pair of Eastern whipbirds.

Dawn turns out its song and feels like a world

    I borrow for a moment, the birds' whip-cry

Chimes the sandstone cliffs and fog, like gloom,

        Rises the eighty metres of waterfall.

Here, like the reeds, I'm helpless

Against the flow, against the gravity pull

Of boulder percussion at its base.

Water, the forest's muse, has tinselled
> The black wattles and honey flowers wet
With webs—like stainglass windows in nature's
> Basilica. I come with mudded boots
To the holy of holies, past the king
Ferns and mat rush to the inner chamber
Of myself. The air is a wet Eden

As if God could be touched through the yellow pea
> Or the scrubwrens' hopscotch in the school yard
Of scribbly gum and sassafras. There's rebirth
> Written in the fur of new banksia leaves—
Baptism for some old parts of the soul.
Next to the path, brown barrels lie like old
Cannons at rest—straight cut, half there

And half here, sepulchres of yesterday.
> The year sheds itself like deadwood, splinters
Of life left behind—as nailed numbers
> On the peppermint trees. A commotion
Of rosellas breaks open the canopy
As I'm called to an altar of water
—Offering alms along Wilde's Meadow creek.

Love is love in place
Sandra Renew

This morning could be the thousandth sun that rises on China's claim of islands and Russia's staking out the Crimea and the moon, gaslighting world geography, geopolitical strategy. Millions move from death and danger, walk up to our own front door. We close our eyes to our complicity in climate change—madmen taunt each other with threats and bombs

under cover

of pandemic panic

global warming

takes a breath—environment

backed into a corner

*

On the concrete walkway between the metal colourbond fences, she drops her bike where the path comes out at the bus stop, settles the boombox onto the grassy edge. The chalk appears, sleight of hand extraction from her bag is part of the cool-move routine. She passes the industrial chalk-stick from hand to hand, faux dancing, then leans down to the concrete and writes, *No masters, no gods* in large, white, rounded letters. She disappears the chalk, hoists the boom-box onto one shoulder, lifts the bike and pedals slowly past the bus-stop, the vibration of the beat still there after the melody disappears

*

Crouching on the rock jutting into the small wetland water hole, she wraps her arms around her knees for warmth, small balloons of breath disappearing into thin air. Shakes the can, quietly, slowly, mixer balls sounding that familiar hollow, muffled rattle. Ducks startle, then zip in a family V formation, out of the reeds into open water, but they don't take off. The can nozzle close to the rock, she writes smoothly, *Love is Love*, hesitates, then punctuates with a heart to the side. Her hair, electric blue against the soft blue of the sky, gleams in the cold sunlight. She waits a moment, watching. Caps the spray can, slides it into her shoulder bag and walks off in the direction of the footbridge

*

There are places where people once gathered which will now remain empty, except for rubbish scuffling in swirling concrete-city whirly-winds. The urban imperative for humans to congregate, meet-up, be social, is on hold. The year rolls on like a badly written movie, plot overdone, marked adult themes, psychological drama, a novel set in someone else's world. Every day the sun goes down. A spot marked on the skyline, moving west in tiny daily increments

unpacking—

unused tickets, pristine credit card

clothes still folded, fresh

COVID puts paid

to dreams and plans

Notes

No gods, no masters is an anarchist and labour slogan. It has been in common use by anarchists in England since the late 19th century

https://www.azlyrics.com Starley Lyrics "Love is Love" on Apple Music

Starley Hope is an Australian singer and song writer who came out as a bisexual in 2017.

morning sickness
Sarah Pearce

    as morning grows loud and close
    i am an unspent arrow

    sickness thrills and breathes
    from extinct to extant

    ask myself how to grow new eyes
    how to name a crisis

    the shrinking does not begin
    it is always underway

    i am visible
    absent consent

    cannot hide myself
    but try to hide my pride

    a different kind of coming out
    etched on the body

Tethered
Rachel Robertson

I knot. Today, triple strand recycled cotton the colour of milky coffee, soft against my fingers, falling from a driftwood branch into easy square knots in alternate rows. Then a curling line of clove hitches, a space of ten centimetres, and another wave-like line. Next, six columns of right-twisting half square knots spinning downwards. Rhythmic, fluid movements, rope and hands making visible the negative spaces between the knots, conjuring patterns in the air.

I knot through lockdown and working from home. I knot through bushfires and floods on the television. I knot through returning to campus, job cuts and hypocrisy. I knot through my son's worsening mental illness. I knot through messages from family and friends in Europe. I knot through radio reports of men harming women and whites harming blacks. I knot through disputes with the National Disability Insurance Scheme.

I weave teal merino wool soumak-style around the vertical rope that hangs between the clove hitch lines, creating a rich layer of colour like water on sand. I run a single line of metallic bronze rope across the wool. It is brazen, almost harsh, against the soft blue-green wool and warm coffee rope. Nothing is simple.

I don't write. Or rather, I write only emails, reports, letters, power point slides, references, lectures, reviews, and academic articles. There is a great emptiness inside me where creativity used to dwell. I understand how lucky I have been, safe here in Western Australia during the pandemic. But still, what I feel is a numbing weight of grief: personal, communal, planetary.

The final rows are a series of switch knots, followed by wrap knots in teal, bundling together each group of four ropes to make the fringe. I unravel the ends, my nails catching in the threads, then trim, brush, and trim again. The wall hanging is done, and for a moment I feel pleasure.

Soon, I will go back into my home office—now a haphazard storeroom for textile, string and fibre—and I will choose some new colours and textures to work with. White rope with black wool and strips of recycled blue sari silk perhaps? Maybe I'll add a band of navy rope or pale green merino? Soon, my fingers will again be making sense of the space. Soon, these knots will hold me in place once more.

Finding Home
Deedle Rodriguez-Tomlinson

> *And I ain't done nothing wrong*
>
> *but I can't find my way back home*
>
> Blind Faith

An island—
one of 7,641
in the Philippines—
the island of Luzon,
my home back home.
An island
ringed all around
with azure waters
that glow in the dark
like the time I walked
along the beach in Anilao
one night and it looked like
a sky full of stars fell to the sea
and gathered along the water's edge.

An island of rivers,
so many of them—
like the Pansipit River
in Batangas, land of mangoes
and sugar canes—
the river that runs
by my cousin's farm in San Nicolas,
the same river where
once, the dead
were ferried to Taal.
The farm they say, is haunted,
inhabited perhaps by spirits
who couldn't find their way home.
This I know to be true—
I felt their eyes on
me the day I visited.
I whispered prayers and pleas to
to please not follow me home.

Today I still live near water—
The Narrows in Brooklyn
—far from my home in the Philippines.
On foggy mornings I sometimes
hear a horn call out, the sound drifting
down the streets of Bay Ridge
from a ship sailing blind in the mist,
going steady as she goes

just hoping to make it to the other side.

Missing
Hazel Smith

the lonely slice of an apple

a phrase with broken teeth

a beheaded intimation

a barrow of rotting tomorrows

a limb google-searching its torso

a view partially blocked by a building

a handful of abandoned almonds

a pitch from the social media song sheet

cracks in the flying buttresses of rhythm

a mood campaigning for insider status

the erratic purring of system and logic

an airborne poem with pink beak, black feathers

a wish that is both clown and chameleon

a discontinuous view of the swaying mountains

lipstick quizzical on a cup

a turned head shaking its locks at foreboding

Viral Year
Hazel Smith

They grew used to stillness and sitting in front of their screens. Became addicted to slow days as if action itself was dawdling.

Communed with flatness and its quirky bursts of undulation.

Welcomed blank calendars, crossed out appointments, overturned deadlines.

Familiar worries shrivelled and withdrew without warning. On standby, but curiously intimidated.

They found that no flood prevents you wading out into art. A darkened cinema dawns from drawn down blinds. A home brew of tea warms the performance. Always the best seats.

Before their attempts at order had been chaotic. Now everything was conscripted onto shelves, drafted into rows. The long arc of the online delivery commandeered the week. Herbs fraternised like thoughts then took their places again, alphabetically arranged.

They kneaded poems, brewed up paintings, slow-baked music.

No fussing over what clothes they wore because their social lives had recoiled. Yet they styled up because now they were doing it for themselves.

Preparing was as good as execution. Planning, the safest form of consumption.

They cooked gourmet meals, pretended they were sitting in the most audacious restaurant.

My Untranquil Mouth
Marion Pym Schaare

A shoulder shrug
    barely there I notice the vibration
        in the reflection of the glass at doors
I pass at midnight
    on my way home
        a hashtag glint

Later the dark lies beneath my eyelids
    & takes flight
            as the morning sun intrudes
        glimmer
            of last year's insights
    hollowed out
        filled in
            a weave of newborn lives
    each year & before
        voices cry

    sweet & petulant
        words hover across the page
          only thoughts yet
      until my pencil pins
        those letters
            shaping verbs into memories running
          freedom an agenda
           born of lockdowns
              unsure transience our only master
            unlike any childhood eyelash play
        my cheek feels hot   my lips burn
    in the fever of forever not.

   Backwards and forwards
      the letters age my grammar
        my mouth a claustrophobic cavern
          where thorns hide
      & out of necessity I smile into quiet.

Cut Flowers
Shannon Sandford

Nonna is waiting outside when I arrive. Shielding her eyes with one hand, the other resting lightly on a large storage container balanced on two wheels. I quickly pull up and shove the tub into the boot of my car, yanking the cargo cover off its velcro hinge to make space. Once she settles into the passenger seat, we wait in long silence for the alarm to engage before setting off down the steep, winding road from her house to the neighbourhood flat. Through cherry limbs bursting with tiny pom-poms that leave scatterings of pink confetti on the ground, past spotlights of yellow wattle poking out from dark shrubbery. Balloon plants hang in mid-air at the end of swooning branches, tiny fists battering the sides of my car as it glides beneath the green skin draped over the world.

We shoot out into the static greys and whites of bubbling suburbia, turning left down the street Nonna likes. She cuts a patch of wild agapanthus from a stranger's yard ... daphne from another's ... hellebores ... pansies ... wintersweet ... something with long antennae ... one that's purple and prickly. A cascade of bristling stems and slick leaves steadily fill the tub, their aroma blending with the damp warmth inside the car. I take a stifling breath and practise holding it until we arrive. Patient and plodding, I follow Nonna along smooth and slippery trails, careful to leave enough space between us. Things feel familiar, despite our absence: the weight of dewy flowers in my arms, soapy-white bore water collected from a dripping tap. But the grass is long and thick now. The sleeping roots of a silver oak have since risen, breaking through the asphalt in sharp fissures.

Macri ... Memoli ... Mengatti ... I look away when Nonna removes her mask and kneels to kiss his gilded picture. Together we push our flowers into oblong vases, disrupting fine layers of dust and cobwebs with violent sloshes of water. It has been a year of many losses, yet I knew eventually we would be drawn back, ceaselessly, to this old grief. My fingers twitch, then falter. I want to hold Nonna's hand. I pick at sparse patches of grass and swirl soil into strange shapes and patterns. Loose petals catch the wind and whirl high above our heads. Like fleeting phantoms borne up towards cerulean sunlight.

How We Live Now
Dominic Symes

these days   I find myself typing poems faster than I can think
there's an art to it   being five minutes early but still apologising for being late
a glitch   like turning on a kettle with no water in it just to watch it rattle   a lag
amidst the chaos your dog moves like a lazy shark between the furniture
last week I covered the clock with a tea towel so that I could concentrate
today you said I miss my work friends but not as much as my actual friends
I watch you leaving with the only valid excuse   (having another zoom call)
it's easy to forget how dangerous a dog is until they're biting a minor celebrity
this is the first year I can properly point to evidence of the seasons changing
maybe this glass of water by your bedside is the most beautiful thing I've ever seen
I'm a bit of a boomer in not trusting the government
but I love all the purple rinse in Extinction Rebellion
some people go years of their lives without anything bad happening to them
which   if you think about it   is a very bourgeois metric of success
I hate the way I look with a beard but feel this strange power in letting things pass
without expending any energy to change them   a form of control maybe?
my silhouette turns out to be just a shadow   (a pretty boring one)
to have always said the right thing   you must think about the past a lot less
to have absolute trust in what will happen next   I imagine
being held guiltlessly in the grip of a benevolent present moment
there's this grass that's grown so long we lose your dog in it
he rustles his way through like a very meagre tornado
before pissing on a tree just as it is coming into bloom

The Gift
after Czeslaw Milosz
Dominic Symes

suddenly the dog isn't fighting other dogs

& when I put the can to my lips
the aluminium groove is uncharacteristically
void of sand

                as if the sun knew that
I wanted to leave the house & so the UV
is less than 6

a mood descends
        as delicate as the ash over Kangaroo Island

& my phone (which I *chose* not to bring with me)
doesn't ring or if it does I don't hear it

a moment   in which the wind gently is buffeting
this shirt which I borrowed   or maybe I inherited
either way I don't think I paid for it

    & none of the buttons need buttoning for now
so I leave them that way

        what do I usually do with my hands?

conscious that I am not touching   anything   for a second

my skin   miraculously   not burnt
maintains contact with the sand
which is cool   as I dig my bare feet in

& honestly it's more than I could have ever hoped for

The Story of the Watch
Amelia Walker

At first, I blamed physical separation for our break-up. Now it's clear, that was inevitable. Distance was a test. We failed. It's okay.

The sorest regrets are things left undone. This isn't always true. But for the story of the watch, *yes*. I mean the wind-up watch I placed on your porch, in a box, with a small metal heart. Really, it's the heart, not the watch, that makes this story—a story of hope that hurts only because I never told you in person, like I dreamed I someday would.

Sharing stories makes them real—lets them travel time, stay alive. Stories never-told weigh like ballast. I need this one free. That you won't hear no longer matters. It's not our story. It's about a man who made a shift precisely when it mattered. It goes like this:

From the start, you and I scrambled for time together. We both worked demanding jobs. Lack of presence was the biggest complaint all my previous lovers lodged. With you, I actually tried. My come-uppance? You cancelled date after date. Facing empty Saturdays, I began cycling country roads, exploring pokey towns. One such venture drew me into a shop run by a man with a curious accent. He'd travelled widely, gathering bespoke items. My eyes fell upon a watch—*the* watch—*your watch*.

'Gift for your boyfriend?' the man asked.

I bobbed my head, indecisive. 'My girlfriend.'

His face contorted; his nostrils flared. I saw him struggle. Then, he straightened up. He cooed, 'These are rare …'

'Yes. And priced accordingly.'

He offered a discount.

'That's still steep … Maybe I'll come back,' I lied, thinking I'd never return.

*

Within weeks, COVID-19 became real. Previously, I'd thought it media hype. Suddenly, shop closures were impending. While neighbours stormed supermarkets for rice and pasta, I cycled for that nowhere town, that funny store.

The man wasn't there. A woman with the same accent served me.

'Are you here for the watch?'

'Yes.'

'My husband told me. You get a discount—and this …'

She produced the heart: a doorknob ornament; tiny; unnecessary, yet purposeful.

I give and receive gifts as messages. The watch was a message. The heart too. As so much closed, one man opened. Although you and I ended, the story of the watch—*the heart*—is finally told. Now it ticks, goes forth, a story of hope:

Prismatic: Fragments, Pieces, Splinters
Annmaree Watharow with Ronnith Morris

Annmaree:

I have deafblindness, meaning the loss of hearing and sight in such combination neither sense can compensate for the other. I experience life as a jigsaw puzzle missing half its pieces, with a few thrown in from other puzzles. I will never see the whole. I labour to extract meaning, but misconstructions are common.

This is unsteady, unpredictable ground on which to navigate a life. Markers are missing or in fragments. For some few, it is complete loss of sight and sound necessitating a touch-centricity for language and life.

For most, it is varying degrees of difficulty accessing information, communicating and being able to orientate and move around the environment. With incomplete information, ordinary life can be hazardous; literally and metaphorically splintered. Unseen stairs—fall traps. To a deafblind pedestrian, unheard cars—near fatal collisions.

And then, how do we narrate our stories? With complex sensory loss comes a multitude of languages signed, spoken and felt. We need aids to storytelling including interpreters, assistive devices, sighted guides, assistance animals and human supports. Collectively we may be dual sensory impaired, but our permutations of needed assistance forms each of us as singular.

These stories—unheard. Told in languages signed, spoken, felt. We need storytelling. Collective. Testimony. Witnessing. Words don't cover these needs.

Ronnith—in conversation with Annmaree:

1. Meaning kaleidoscopes, freewheels, concertinas, then expands—erroneously sometimes. In modes comic and tragic. Gallant. Sometimes meaning struts, slips. Sometimes sense becomes word salad. That's the deafblind prism. See the whole. Never. Feel the whole—fortuitously. Extract meaning—making it out of mettle.

2. Cartography: consider it landmarking. Wayfinding. Making ground to navigate life. My markers sight and sound. The other marker—touch—for language and through language, life's integral. But touch also makes us social, communal. Not. So. Isolated. Grounds for path-making. Haptic. Somatic. Communal. Civilised.

3. Experience is not uniform, not ever uniform, often unheard, unacknowledged. Needs are individual. Are you more blind than deaf? is a meaningless question. So is, Are you more deaf than blind? Recognition is re-cognition.

4. Your chances of having hearing loss and vision loss and dual sensory impairment increase markedly as you age.

In times of social distancing, experience is even more unfeeling and unfelt. This has been a time of unmaking. Difficult for us all, especially for the frail, the elderly, the institutionalised.

Deafblind experiences are dealt in fragments, pieces and splinters. Prismatic. These narratives are compelling.

Another step in the cycle
Jen Webb

Your heart, beating, while the world is practicing Buteyko breathing, and a skink has found the sticks we propped in the birdbath and is hauling itself hand over hand away from death. The kid next door is playing scales on an alto horn, I can hear his quick intake of air between C sharp and E. Practice, his mother says, practice. Your heart, a metronome, beats out three-four time at a steady middle C, and the kid next door misses a note, honks off key. If you were awake you'd laugh no doubt or cross the fence to correct his stance. You breathe on; deep sounds, slow sounds; sounds the world makes as it moves into the next difficult pose, murmurs *omm*.

Back to where we started from
Jen Webb

We took the challenge, and within weeks were at the doctors, running on their machines, gasping *too fast too hard* while the nurses said *run, bitch, make it count*. Next we took an easier approach, eating turmeric for breakfast, smearing coconut oil on our skin. Do I smell weird, we asked each other and each said no, you smell fine. 'I wish our lives were more urbane,' you said, but we both know that's not likely. *Dark strangers are coming your way,* said the fortune teller, *but they're not the good looking kind.* She folded our palms closed, refused our coins. Now we are putting all our energy into paying down the mortgage, putting out the bins on time. This is not the life we imagined we'd be living; but we're living it.

The Tea-Room, First Day Back
Rose Williamson

Loud Sandals walks past me and opens the part of her face that makes the sound of greeting and the corridor becomes a wind tunnel of toothpaste and morning soap. 'Hello,' I say too late for Sandals but the fridge in the tea-room shines in a pleased sort of way and the kettle winks. 'Nice to see you again.'

Bench, tea-bags, coffee plunger, sink, taps, cupboards, cups. I careen between them before remembering the hand sanitiser, which is over by the door. Bugger. On the way, my foot bangs itself on a chair and blood seeps from under a toenail. No matter. What's worse is that the nozzle on the squirty bottle has clogged up so when I push down the sanitiser sprays my face and a bit gets into my eye.

Jovial Shirt marches through the door and when we see each other up close, we push apart like the same poles on two magnets. We both open the parts of our faces that make the sound of greeting, but nothing comes out although my injuries give me a good excuse. Loud Sandals re-appears. She strides into the tea-room and springs back too before hovering between me and Jovial Shirt. They both want to use the squirty bottle and I listen to myself explain its malfunction as my sleeved arms wipe off the goo (avoid touching your face with your fingers!). All the while, there's an eye dance going on—theirs with mine, theirs with each other.

The sign on the wall says eight persons are allowed in the tea-room at any one time. Surely that means persons of a personable type. I open the part of my face that also makes the sound of farewell. 'See you later,' I say too late and low for Loud Sandals and Jovial Shirt, but the corridor into which I seep antiseptic and sweat hears and is none too pleased. Turn right, then left into my office, shut and lock the door. I lie down on the rug, next to the little pile of mouse droppings, and close my stinging eye, then the other.

(Un) Certainty
Miriam Wei Wei Lo

beach

We thought we were the concrete piles
beneath the jetty: weather-proof,
holding up the boards, home
to fanworms and sponges,
circled by schools of glittering fish.

But all this time
                we were the teenaged boys
          on the red pontoon,
              attempting handstands
in the south-west chop,
                      unable to hold our positions
    for longer than a minute.

tomorrow

as porous as bleached coral washed up on the shore

as tenuous as the line between sick and well

as open as the rift between here and gone

will it survive?

will it?

still

the posture of prayer

hands open

knees on the towel

south-west breeze picking up sand in tiny eddies

slightly ridiculous

lips moving beneath my face-mask
like I could be talking
to an invisible God.

I could be talking
to an invisible God.

Leaving Lockdown: My Wish for You
Kimberly K. Williams

I know I left
my hair behind
(I always do)—

strands of it
woven through-
out our brief

life. I hope
you encounter it
tucked under

a pillow when
you sleep, find
it trapped in

the carpet when
you clean, curled
against the bottom

cabinet when
you sweep. I hope
you discover my

blonde tendrils
coiled in your back-
seat or threaded

through the fly-
screen (floating
inside &

outside at one
time), drifting along-
side the pool

or tangled in
& around the potted
lemon tree leaves.

Ode: Facing the Light
Dugald Williamson

The isolation is a hurt, the way
it undoes things before they are.
Try again for a break on the job front,
and the philosophical propositions,
not to mention, on language and pain.
Neither is poetry banished
in the dawn sky, for what's more
sociable than a single star.
You call early. Any joy yet?
In the background, a little staccato,
and from a tree near your house
rosellas glide in the curve of a bind,
to a coda by the gate—as we speak,
an envoi, the makings of a jar.

A Letter in Autumn
Dugald Williamson

The morning star,
like a fallen note from a prelude,
good save by the bellbird.

She listens,
making sense of the fact,
dawning diagnosis.

A few bare outlines
give definition
to the new light on things.

A lustre draws breath on vines,
she stores it for you, and writes,
a leaf in Epicurean vein,

something imaginable,
a different presence,
to be in company again,

staying the unknown distance.
Look, last apples out on a limb
windfall to a green apron.

The Seventh Day
Christina Yin

On the seventh day after his passing, I wait for my father to visit me.

It is seventeen weeks after the Movement Control Order is decreed on 18th May throughout Malaysia, the lockdown to prevent the spread of the coronavirus, COVID-19 that is killing the unprepared and unsuspecting. I am in my parents' home in Petaling Jaya, having left Kuching, Sarawak where I started a life with my husband twenty-five years ago.

People warn us that loved ones who have left will come back on the seventh day. Lay out their favourite food and drink, earthly things they enjoyed, they tell us. Always, it is told as a warning, as if we should fear their return, that they will be angry. But I am not afraid. I know my father loves me and would never hurt me. I hope my father will visit me tonight.

We leave for him a shot of his favourite single malt whisky and Lays sour cream and onion crisps on the coffee table beside the sofa he loved to lie on to watch the news or football on TV.

In the morning, the food and drink are untouched, but my husband had dreamed of him on a travellator, neither sad nor ill, just moving away. Our younger daughter, Emily, in Iowa City dreamed of him walking down the slope near Blessed Sacrament Church as she walked up on the other side of the road. 'I'm sorry I couldn't be there with you,' Emily told him. Her grandfather said it was okay, relieving Emily of the guilt she feels for isolating in her college apartment, unable to make her way home through a labyrinth of flights across America and international borders that are shutting down.

My father left us on 10th July 2020 in the early months of the pandemic. We had been battling the virus on one front and the disease that was relentlessly gripping him on another. Each day, he ate and drank less. The doctors tried different medical procedures, but the disease kept telling his body not to eat and drink.

I am home in Kuching now with my husband. Katie, our eldest, is in Glasgow and Emily in Iowa City. My mother lives alone in Petaling Jaya. The pandemic persists, but we are moving on, somehow.

The seventh day is long past, but I still hope my father will visit me.

Bio notes

Alberta Natasia Adji is currently a PhD candidate at Edith Cowan University, Australia. Her research focuses on the intersection between life writing and the genre of autobiographical novel. She has published refereed articles in various scholarly journals, including *Women: A Cultural Review, Journal of Graphic Novels and Comics, Prose Studies, Life Writing,* and *Cinder*. She has also published a short story in *Meniscus* and a piece of flash fiction in *The Incompleteness Book* (2020).

Eugen Bacon is African Australian, a computer scientist mentally reengineered into creative writing. Her work has won, been shortlisted, longlisted or commended in national and international awards, including the BSFA Awards, Bridport Prize, Copyright Agency Prize, Australian Shadows Awards, Ditmar Awards and Nommo Award for Speculative Fiction by Africans. Her newest collection, *Danged Black Thing*, is out with Transit Lounge Publishing in November 2021. Website: eugenbacon.com / Twitter: @EugenBacon

My poetry is published under the name of Therese, and I'm otherwise known as **Roxanne Bodsworth**. I am a poet, celebrant, and farmer living in Northeast Victoria. In 2020, I completed my PhD through Victoria University with a feminist reconstruction of Irish mythology using a hybrid combination of poetry and prose. My verse novel, *The Tangled Web*, was published in 1989 by Openbook Publishers, and the third edition of my nonfiction book, *Sunwyse—Celebrating the Wheel of the Year in Australia*, was released this year. Widely published in a range of genres, writing keeps me sane (almost).

Donna Lee Brien, PhD, is Emeritus Professor of Creative Industries at Central Queensland University, Australia. Author, co-author and editor of 23 books including *Writing the Australian Beach: Local Site, Global Idea* (2020), *The Shadow Side of Nursing: Paradox, Image and Identity* (2020), *Publishing and Culture* (2019), *Offshoot: Contemporary Lifewriting Methodologies and Practice* (2018) and *Recovering History Through Fact and Fiction* (2017), Donna co-edits *The Australasian Journal of Popular Culture*. In 2021, Donna began studying for her second doctorate, writing the biography of Bondi Beach.

Didem Caia is a writer, dramaturge, theatre maker and arts leader from Melbourne. A graduate of NIDA and VCA, Didem is currently a PhD candidate in the School of Media and Communications at RMIT. Didem is a 2021 UN Global Voices Scholar, a Melbourne Fringe Festival 2021 Emerging Playwright commission awardee, and is on the board of celebrated literary journal, *Going Down Swinging*.

Aidan Coleman has published three collections of poetry, most recently *Mount Sumptuous* (Wakefield Press, 2020). Besides poetry, he writes essays, reviews and Shakespeare textbooks and he is currently completing a biography, *Thin Ice: A Life of John Forbes* to be published by Melbourne UP in late 2022. Aidan is an Early Career Researcher at the J.M. Coetzee Centre for Creative Practice at the University of Adelaide.

Shady Cosgrove is the author of *What the Ground Can't Hold* (Picador, 2013) and *She Played Elvis* (Allen and Unwin, 2009). Her short works have appeared in *Best Australian Stories, Overland, Antipodes, Southerly*, and Spineless Wonders anthologies. She teaches creative writing at the University of Wollongong, Australia.

Lynn Davidson's latest poetry collection *Islander* is published by Shearsman Books, Bristol, and Victoria University Press, Wellington. She had a Hawthornden Fellowship in 2013 and a Bothy Project Residency at Inshriach Bothy in the Cairngorms in 2016. In 2011 she was Visiting Artist at Massey University. She won Poetry New Zealand's 2020 Poetry Award, and is the 2021 Randell Cottage Writer in Residence. Lynn has a Doctorate in Creative Writing and teaches creative writing. She recently returned to New Zealand after four years living and writing in Edinburgh.

Dave Drayton was an amateur banjo player, founding member of the Atterton Academy, and the author of *E, UIO, A: a feghoot* (Container), *A pet per ably-faced kid* (Stale Objects dePress), *P(oe)Ms* (Rabbit), *Haiturograms* (Stale Objects dePress), and *Poetic Pentagons* (Spacecraft Press).

Katrina Finlayson is a creative writer and researcher, working mostly in creative nonfiction. Katrina's personal and critical essays have been published in *Meanjin, TEXT* and *Axon*. Her writing explores ideas about strangeness, place and displacement, home and travel, and the nature and significance of memory and identity.

Jane Frank is a Brisbane poet, originally from Maryborough in the Fraser Coast region, and the author of *Wide River* (Calanthe Press, 2020). Her work has been recognised in awards and widely published and anthologised. Most recently, her poems have appeared in *Westerly, StylusLit, Takahē, Shearsman* and *Live Encounters*, and are forthcoming in a number of anthologies including *Not Very Quiet: The Anthology* (Recent Work Press, 2021), *Poetry for the Planet* (Litoria Press, 2021) and *Grieve vol 9* (Hunter Writer's Centre, 2021). She has a PhD in cultural studies and teaches creative and professional writing at Griffith University.

In addition to publishing several commercial books as a ghost writer, project writer and project editor, **Laura Fulton's** creative and critical work has appeared in publications including *Swamp Writing, TEXT, Qualitative Inquiry, Pendulum Papers* and *The Incompleteness Book Part I*. Her current novel in progress addresses themes of disruption, longing and loss through the epistolary voice and the imagined family history, how we cope with those experiences and ways of looking forward and back.

Stephanie Green publishes short fiction, poetry and travel essays in Australian and international journals. Her most recent book is a collection of prose poems, *Breathing in Stormy Seasons* (Recent Work Press 2019). Her poetry is included in anthologies such as the *Anthology of Australian Prose Poetry* (Hetherington & Atherton, 2020). She publishes extensively as a research scholar, recently contributing to *Text Journal Special Issue 56: Re-mapping Travel Writing* (October 2019), which she co-edited with Nigel Krauth and Stefan Jatschka, and *The Routledge Companion to Australian Literature* (Gildersleeve, 2020).

Rebecca Hamilton is a second-year Creative Practice PhD student in the School of the Arts & Media at the University of New South Wales. Rebecca previously completed a Bachelor of Writing with First Class Honours at the University of Canberra, where she also received the Dean's Excellence Award. She is an experienced editor who has worked with a number of major publishing companies, including Pan Macmillan, Hachette and Murdoch Books. Some of the titles she has worked on include Behrouz Boochani's award-winning *No Friend but the Mountains* (2018), and Amani Haydar's forthcoming *The Mother Wound* (2021).

Thomas Hamlyn-Harris is an illustrator and writer of comics, visual narrative and short fiction. His work has been published in games, magazines, children's fiction, nonfiction and anthologies, including *ACE II*.

Dominique Hecq is a poet, fiction writer and scholar. She grew up in the French-speaking part of Belgium and now lives in Melbourne. Hecq writes across genres and sometimes across tongues. Her works include a novel, three collections of short stories and ten books of poetry. Among other honours, Hecq is a recipient of the 2018 International Best Poets Prize administered by the International Poetry Translation and Research Centre in conjunction with the International Academy of Arts and Letters, and 'Smacked' was runner up in the 2021 Carmel Bird Digital Literary Award (Spineless Wonders). *Tracks* (Recent Work Press, 2020) and *Songlines* (Hedgehog Poetry Press, 2021) are her latest books of poetry. With Eugen Bacon, she co-authored *Speculate: A Collection of Microlit* (Meerkat Press, 2021).

Paul Hetherington is a distinguished poet who has published numerous full-length poetry and prose poetry collections and has won or been nominated for more than thirty national and international awards and competitions. He won the 2021 Bruce Dawe National Poetry Prize, and the 2014 West Australian Premier's Book Awards (poetry). Paul is Professor of Writing in the Faculty of Arts and Design at the University of Canberra, head of the International Poetry Studies Institute (IPSI) and joint founding editor of the international online journal *Axon: Creative Explorations*. He founded the International Prose Poetry Group in 2014. He is co-author of a scholarly study of the prose poem for Princeton University Press (2020), and co-editor of the *Anthology of Australian Prose Poetry* (MUP, 2020).

Christine Howe is a writer and academic who works across various genres—novels, poetry, microfiction and essays. Her first novel, *Song in the Dark*, was published by Penguin. Christine's prose poetry has been included in a number of Spineless Wonders anthologies and her poetry, essays and scholarly works have been published in journals such as the *Griffith Review*; *Island*; *Cordite*; *Law, Text, Culture*; and *TEXT*.

Anita Jawary is a Melbourne writer, poet and artist. She has worked as a freelance journalist, teacher and academic and is now retired. Her passions are good writing, good art, and exploring the fork in the tree where they meet.

A journalist for more than forty years, **Sue Joseph** (PhD) began teaching print journalism and creative writing, particularly creative nonfiction writing, at the University of Technology Sydney from 1997. Now as Associate Professor, she holds an Adjunct position at Avondale University, is a Senior Research Fellow at the University of South Australia and is a doctoral supervisor at the University of Sydney, Central Queensland University and the UTS. She is currently Joint Editor of *Ethical Space: The International Journal of Communication Ethics*, and Special Issues Co-Editor of *TEXT: Journal of Writing and Writing Courses*.

Daniel Juckes is a writer from Perth, Western Australia. He is a Lecturer in Creative Writing at UWA, and he holds a PhD in Creative Writing from Curtin University. His creative and critical work has been published in journals such as *Axon, Life Writing*, M/C Journal, *TEXT* and *Westerly*, and his research investigates seamlessness in prose style and the potential of objects in stories about the past.

Helena Kadmos is a Lecturer in English Literature at the University of Notre Dame, Fremantle Campus. Her research explores the capacities of short fiction and creative non-fiction to explore the quotidian of women's lives.

Dean Kerrison is a PhD candidate at Griffith University working on his first novel. His work often focuses on the (dis)connection of the outsider in foreign lands. He's had fiction, nonfiction along with a playscript and poetry published in *TEXT Journal, Meniscus, The Bangalore Review, Joao Roque Literary Journal, The Lit Quarterly, Allegory Ridge*, and others.

Jeri Kroll is Emeritus Professor of English and Creative Writing at Flinders University and an Adjunct Professor Creative Arts at Central Queensland University. *Vanishing Point* (verse novel) was shortlisted for the 2015 Queensland Literary Awards. A George Washington University stage adaptation was a winner in the 47th Kennedy Center American College Theatre Festival. Recent critical books are *Creative Writing: Drafting, Revising and Editing* (2020), *'Old and New, Tried and Untried': Creativity and Research in the 21st Century University* (2016), and Research Methods in Creative Writing (2013). She is a Doctor of Creative Arts candidate at University of Wollongong.

Joshua Lobb is Senior Lecturer in Creative Writing at the University of Wollongong. His stories have appeared in *The Bridport Prize Anthology, Best Australian Stories, Animal Studies Journal, Griffith Review, Plumwood Mountain, Text* and *Southerly*. His 'novel in stories' about grief and climate change, *The Flight of Birds* (Sydney University Press, 2019) was shortlisted for the 2019 Readings Prize for New Australian Fiction and the 2020 Mascara Literary Review Avant Garde Awards for Best Fiction. He is also part of the multi-authored project, *100 Atmospheres: Studies in Scale and Wonder* (Open Humanities Press, 2019).

Miriam Wei Wei Lo writes poetry to explore human experience and to celebrate the creative capacity of language. She teaches creative writing at Sheridan Institute. She is of mixed Malaysian-Chinese and Anglo-Australian descent and lives, with her extended family, in the Walyalup (Fremantle) area. Follow her @miriamweiweilo on Insta.

Rose Lucas is a Melbourne poet and academic at Victoria University. She has three collections of poetry: *Even in the Dark* (UWAP, 2013), *Unexpected Clearing* (UWAP, 2016) and *This Shuttered Eye* (Girls on Key, 2021). Her forthcoming collection is *Increments of the Everyday* (Puncher & Wattman, 2022). 'Year of Breath' comes from a collaborative exhibition she did with visual artist Sharon Monagle, 2020 Shelter in Place (April 2021).

Gay Lynch works as an adjunct academic at Flinders University, Adelaide, publishing essays, hybrid memoir pieces, novels, papers and short stories. Recent works include *Unsettled* (2019), an Australian frontier novel, and essays and stories in *Best Australian Stories, Bluestem Journal, Edições Humus Limitada, Glimmer Press, Island, Meanjin, Meniscus, Griffith Review, Westerly, Recent Work Press, TEXT* and *Sleepers Almanac*.

Mario Daniel Martín is an Honorary Associate Professor in Spanish at ANU. As a creative writer, he has published 12 books (short stories, poetry, children's novels, science fiction), and more than 60 individually published short stories, theatre plays and poems. He has written the scripts for 5 performed theatre plays, 3 radio plays and 3 films. Most of his creative work has been published in the Spanish-speaking world.

Mia McAuslan is a writer and researcher living on Dja Dja Wurrung and Taungurung Country. She writes about homesickness and eco-anxiety. Her work has been shortlisted for the Rachel Funari Prize for Fiction, the Overland VU Short Story Prize, and longlisted for the Richell Prize by Hachette Australia.

Sam Meekings is an Assistant Professor of Creative Writing at Northwestern University in Qatar. With Marshall Moore, is the co-editor of *The Place and the Writer: International Intersections of Teacher Lore and Creative Writing Pedagogy* (Bloomsbury, 2021). He is the author of *Under Fishbone Clouds* (called 'a poetic evocation of the country and its people' by the New York Times), *The Book of Crows*, and *The Afterlives of Dr Gachet*. He has a PhD in Creative Writing from Lancaster University and has taught writing at NYU and the University of Chichester in the UK.

Peta Murray is an Australian writer-performer and late blooming paracademic in the School of Media and Communication at RMIT University in Melbourne. Her experience as a dramaturge and theatre-maker informs her work as practice-led researcher. Peta is interested in the application of transdisciplinary and arts-based practices as modes of inquiry and as forms of cultural activism, and her current focus is the collaborative possibilities of artful ethnography.

Lili Pâquet is a Lecturer in Writing at the University of New England with an interest in rhetoric, crime fiction, and digital writing and publishing.

Dr Sarah Pearce is a poet, performer and academic from Tarndanya/Adelaide, Australia. Her work appears in *Aeternum, Outskirts, Meniscus, writing from below* and *TEXT*. She has held residencies at Adelaide City Library and FELTspace gallery, and performed at Blenheim Festival and Adelaide Fringe Festival. Her writing concerns the body, the self, points of connection, the Gothic, queer identity and experiences of mental ill health and distress.

Mary Pomfret writes short stories and poems and her work has been published widely in anthologies and literary journals including *Meniscus* and *The Incompleteness Book*. Her debut novel 'The Hard Seed ' was published in 2018. Mary lives and works in Bendigo, Australia. In 2016, La Trobe University awarded Mary a doctorate in English for her creative thesis on generational trauma.

Julia Prendergast's novel, *The Earth Does Not Get Fat* was published in 2018 (UWA Publishing: Australia). Her short stories feature in the current edition of *Australian Short Stories*. Other stories have been recognised and published: *Lightship Anthology 2* (UK), *Glimmer Train* (US), *TEXT* (AU), *Séan Ó Faoláin Competition* (IE). Julia's research is practice-led: exploring creative writing through theories from neuropsychoanalysis. Julia is a Senior Lecturer (Writing and Literature) and Academic Director Pathways and Partnerships, at Swinburne University, Melbourne. She is Chair of the Australasian Association of Writing Programs (AAWP), the peak academic body representing the discipline of Creative Writing in Australasia.

Peter Ramm is a poet and teacher who writes on the Gundungarra lands of the NSW Southern Highlands. He has won the South Coast Writer's Centre Poetry Award and the Harri Jones Memorial Prize, and has shortlisted for the Bridport, ACU, Blake, and Newcastle Poetry Prizes. Peter has recently published poems with *Cordite, Westerly, Plumwood Mountain,* and *Eureka Street Journal*. He finds inspiration in the landscape and people of Southeastern NSW.

Sandra Renew's poetry is published in Australia in *Griffith Review, Canberra Times, Hecate, Axon, Australian Poetry Journal*. Her poetry collections are *It's the sugar, Sugar* (Recent Work Press, 2021); *Acting Like a Girl* (Recent Work Press,

2019); and *The Orlando Files* (Ginninderra Press, 2018). Sandra's collection, *Acting Like a Girl*, won the 2020 ACT Writing and Publishing Award for Poetry.

Rachel Robertson is Associate Professor in the School of Media, Creative Arts and Social Inquiry at Curtin University. Her research interests include life writing, creative nonfiction, the literary essay and disability studies.

Deedle Rodriguez-Tomlinson was born and raised in the Philippines. Her essay on her experience during COVID-19 lockdown was published in the 2020 Australasian Association of Writing Programs special issue *TEXT: The In/completeness of Human Experience*. Her poems, reflecting her peripatetic life, have appeared in the literary issue of *Silliman University Journal*, and *Tomas*, the University of Santo Tomas literary journal, both in the Philippines. One of her poems is also included in Under the Storm: An Anthology of Contemporary Philippine Poetry. She lives in Brooklyn with her husband Tim.

Shannon Sandford is a PhD candidate and casual academic in the College of Humanities, Arts, and Social Sciences at Flinders University, South Australia. Her research background is in Life Narrative, with particular interest in trauma writing, 'autographics' and comics studies. She is a member of the Flinders Life Narrative Research Group.

Marion Pym Schaare, a Brisbane-based linguist, poet, short story writer and author, has works published in a variety of poetry anthologies, magazines and journals. Awarded the Robyn Mathison Poetry Award (2017), and a place in the *ACU anthology* (2019), publications in *Scope, Neithor/Nor, The Blue Nib, Our Inside Voices*, and (publications in press) *Hecate*, and the *QLD Memories Anthology*, stand as several milestones for her.

Hazel Smith is a poet, performer and multimedia artist and Emeritus Professor at Western Sydney University. She has published four volumes of poetry including *Word Migrants* (Giramondo, 2016); several academic and pedagogical books, including *The Contemporary Literature-Music Relationship* (Routledge, 2016), and numerous performance, installation and multimedia works. She is a member of austraLYSIS, the sound and intermedia arts group, has performed and presented her work extensively internationally, and has been commissioned by the ABC to write several works for radio. In 2018 she was, with Will Luers and Roger Dean, awarded first place in the US-based Electronic Literature Organisation's Robert Coover prize for the work *novelling*. Her website is at www.australysis.com

Dominic Symes lives and writes on Wurundjeri Country in Naarm (Melbourne). His poetry and criticism have appeared in *Overland, Cordite, Australian Book Review, Australian Poetry Journal*, and *Axon: Creative Explorations*, among others. He is the editor for reviews at *TEXT Journal*.

Amelia Walker has published four poetry collections, most recently *Dreamday* (Campbelltown Arthouse, 2017. From 2017-2019), she served as secretary on the AAWP executive board. She is presently employed on a teaching-only contract at a South Australian university.

Annmaree Watharow, a medical doctor, recently completed a PhD on the deafblind experience in hospital. She has written of being a deafblind researcher and is interested in narrative medicine, disability writing and disability activism. Ronnith Morris taught Annmaree Narrative Writing in 2014, and is lucky to be her friend.

Jen Webb is Distinguished Professor of Creative Practice at the University of Canberra, and co-editor of the literary journal *Meniscus* and scholarly journal *Axon: Creative Explorations*. She researches and writes about suffering and resilience. Her most recent poetry collections are *Moving Targets* (Recent Work Press, 2018), and *Flight Mode* (with Shé Hawke; Recent Work Press 2020).

Kimberly K. Williams is an HDR PhD student at University of Canberra writing a poetry thesis on poetic form and the re-collection of nineteenth-century women's voices in America. She has published two books of poems: *Finally, the Moon*, from Stephen F Austin University Press (2017), and *Sometimes a Woman*, from Recent Work Press (2021).

Dugald Williamson is a Professor at the University of New England, Armidale NSW, where he works in media, communication and writing studies. His poetry has appeared in various journals including *Australian Poetry Journal, Meanjin, Southerly, TEXT* and *Westerly*.

Rose Williamson is a Senior Lecturer in Writing at University of New England (UNE), Armidale, NSW.

Dr Christina Yin lives in Sarawak, Malaysian Borneo with her husband, children and two mixed-breed dogs. Formerly a news anchor, journalist and communications officer in a conservation organisation, she is now a writer and Senior Lecturer at Swinburne University of Technology, Sarawak Campus. Her work has appeared in *Anak Sastra, eTropic Journal, New Writing* and *TEXT Journal*, among others.